THE PSALTER
IN THE
TEMPLE AND THE CHURCH

THE PSALTER
IN THE
TEMPLE AND THE CHURCH

"From the beginning knowledge
of God is the dowry of the soul."
Tertullian

by

Marie Pierik

Author of
The Spirit of Gregorian Chant
The Song of the Church
Gregorian Chant Analyzed and Studied

The Catholic University of America Press
Washington 17, D. C.
1957

Nihil Obstat:
    Russell Woolen
    Censor Deputatus

Imprimatur:
    ✠ Patrick A. O'Boyle
    Archbishop of Washington
November 16, 1956

PREFACE

Some time ago while I was teaching in a Trappistine monastery, I picked out a large edition of a study of the Bible from a bookcase in the guest quarters where I was housed. At first I started to read casually, then gradually I became so absorbed in new knowledge of the "Book of Books," that from then on I spent practically every free moment of my stay at the monastery perusing the pages of this magnificent volume.

Heretofore I had unwittingly felt that normal versification in the New Testament, daily association with the Psalms, and the amount of Old Testament Scripture used in the Mass and the Divine Office as the liturgy unfolds in the life of Christ and the Church during the course of the liturgical cycle, constituted "knowledge of Holy Scripture." Now I realized that more complete insight into the tremendous religious dramas of the Old Testament meant deeper penetration into, and appreciation of, the New Testament, fulfilment of the Old. And I began to wonder whether there were not other Catholics active in Church labor who had felt as I did, that knowledge of Holy Scripture does not necessarily include adequate familiarity with the Old Testament in its entirety.

Some months later, while I was accumulating material on the Bible and setting it down in writing, I needed to be apprised of certain facts bearing on current Scriptural labor. After appealing to several sources, from which I received no definite answer, the thought came to mind that a member of the Catholic Biblical Association of America might be willing to accord me the information I was seeking. So somewhat hesitantly I sent my queries to their general office in Washington, D. C.

Great was my surprise and delight when, shortly after, I received a full-paged typed letter more than answering my questions, written by none other than the Executive Secretary of the Biblical Association, the Chairman of the Editorial Board for the new translation of the Holy Bible—Reverend Louis F. Hartman, C.Ss.R.

In the face of such gracious condescension on the part of an eminent biblical scholar for a mere dilettante in the specialized subject she was treating, I started to approach Father Hartman from time to time for necessary enlightenment, although, I will admit, with a prayer on my lips that the patience of a man dedicated to the most exigent of labors in his own field, would not be exhausted at my seeming importunity. But even though this might well have been the case, there was never a sign of this in the masterly and complete explanations sent back to me.

Eventually I concentrated on the Psalter, a territory in which, as a student of the Chant, I felt at home. But even here, in exploring the Psalms in their various phases, I discovered that despite the fact that they had carried me through "thick and thin" now for some decades, there was much in their vital history and profound content which had escaped me, and which was of too illuminating and inspirational a nature to appropriate for personal benefit alone.

So that is the story behind this short study, in which I hope to have shared with others something, if only a glimpse, of the tremendous power and unfathomable beauty embodied in the most divinely inspired odes which have ever come to light— songs which hover between heaven and earth—the Psalter of the Temple and the Church.

MARIE PIERIK

ACKNOWLEDGEMENTS

We are particularly indebted to The Grail Press, St. Meinrad, Indiana, for their generosity in furnishing the plates for Part Two of this study.

We wish also to acknowledge our gratitude to the following persons and organizations for the privilege of using valuable knowledge contained in their publications:

Bloch Publishing Co., New York; the Catholic Biblical Quarterly, Washington, D. C.; Desclée & Cie., Tournai, Rome; les Editions du Cerf, Paris; Funk & Wagnalls Co., New York; the Gilmary Society, New York; H. Holt & Co., New York; F.E.C. Leukart, Breslau; the Macmillan Company, New York; Pontifical Biblical Institute, Rome; Publications for Judaism, Cincinnati; St. Anthony Guild, Paterson, N. J.; the Soncino Press, London; Joseph F. Wagner, New York.

CONTENTS

Part I

THE PSALTER IN THE TEMPLE

Part II

ILLUSTRATIONS

PART I

THE PSALTER IN THE TEMPLE

Chapter I

THE PSALTER

The word Psalter means a stringed instrument and then by transference a collection of songs.

In rabbinical literature the designation of the Book of Psalms is *Sefer Tehillim*, the "Book of Praises," and this name has passed into traditional usage among Jews, although only one Psalm, 144 (Hebrew 145), has the word *tehillah* (praise) in its superscription. This triumphant hymn of praise, calling on all men to glorify the majesty and greatness of God, inaugurates the concluding group, which rounds up the Psalter with a series of hymns of praise, reaching its climax in the superb *Alleluia* of Psalm 150.

Not only the songs of praise, but the entire collection of Psalms made up a manual for the Temple service, chiefly one of praise. The Septuagint, an old Greek version of the Old Testament reputed to have been made by *seventy* translators, gave the collection the name *Psalterion* (stringed instrument); the Vulgate, *Liber Psalmorum*; the Council of Trent, *Psalterium*; and to designate a number of poems called in Hebrew "songs or chants," the LXX employs the word *psalmos*—hence the name Psalter and Psalm.

When referring to Psalms included in the Jewish liturgy, the Talmudic authorities mention them as "verses of praise," employing the Aramaic term *zimra*, which is cognate with the Hebrew *mizmor* (found in the heading of fifty-seven Psalms), Septuagint *psalmos*, Vulgate *canticum*. So both in Hebrew and Greek the root meaning is to play instrumental music, and then to sing to musical accompaniment.

1

That, in effect, explains the origin of most of the compositions of the Psalter. The singing of hymns by a choir of Levites and by the assembly and worshippers, with an accompaniment of string and wind instruments, was a feature of the religious service of the Temple. A number of Psalms present clear evidence of this liturgical use and were associated with days of the week or with festival occasions by a tradition that is independently attested both by the LXX and the Talmud, the body of Jewish civil and canonical law not to be found in the Pentateuch (Cf. p. 5). However, it does not follow that all the Psalms were so employed; in fact, some of them would scarcely be suitable for the purpose.

In the Masoretic text (the record, committed to memory, of the rabbinical teachings as to the form and reading of the Hebrew Bible) the Psalter heads the third division of the Hebrew Bible, the Hagiographa, or "Writings." In the Talmud the order is given as Ruth, Psalms, etc. In the Greek Bible, it has occupied various positions, but ordinarily is placed first. In the Vulgate, the Book of Psalms occupies second place, after Job, among the Sapiential Books.[1]

In the Synagogue the Psalter may be fairly described as the "Hymnal of the Temple." In the Church, the Psalms have always been the chief source of liturgical prayer, particularly in the Proper of the Mass, and are especially appointed in the Breviary for daily recital of the clergy.

Concerning the doctrine of inspiration in the Psalms, the Catholic view has regard to the Psalms as they now stand in the Canon and does not impede a Catholic from admitting various redactions of the Psalter previous to our present redaction; in fact, even uninspired liturgical redactions of the Psalms would not be contrary to what the Church teaches in the matter of inspiration, so long as the redactor had preserved intact and absolutely unaltered the inspired meaning of the text.[2]

2

Numbering of the Psalms

In both the Hebrew, and the Latin Vulgate the number of the Psalms is 150. However, the application of the numbers in each differs. Neither numbering is preferable to the other. In early manuscripts the separation of the Psalms was not indicated, and this fact explains the differences in division in the Septuagint, which the Vulgate follows, and in the present Hebrew Bible. The Biblical Commission (May 1, 1910) explains the numerical variance between the Hebrew and Latin texts as follows:

Certain Psalms, whether by David or by other authors, have, for liturgical reasons, been divided or even welded together. Further, we can hold that some Psalms, for example, the *Miserere* (50, H. 51), have, for the sake of better adaptability to historical circumstances or Jewish festivals, been slightly remolded or modified, either by the removal or addition of one or two verses, without detriment to the whole text.[3]

The diversity in numbering between the LXX and Vulgate and the Masoretic text is portrayed in the following tabulation:

LXX and Vulgate	Masoretic Text
1–8	1–8
9	9–10
10–112	11–113
113	114–115
114–115	116
116–145	117–146
146–147	147
148–150	148–150[4]

Division of the Psalter

The collection of the Psalms, as we have it, is very old, but cannot go back beyond the Captivity (588–538), as in it are some Psalms which clearly were written either during or after the period of exile, as, for example, Psalms 84 (85), 105 (106),

3

136 (137). It would seem that the Psalter must have been closed in the period of Esdras,[5] or not much later. There is an increasing tendency among biblical exegetes of today to assign an earlier date to the poems which some scholars would consider as coming from the Maccabean age.[6]

At first the Psalms existed as separate pieces and then small collections were made, probably for liturgical use. The existence of primitive collections which preceded our present five books cannot be denied. However, the actual contents of some of these earlier collections are often problematic.

The process of making these collections was in three stages:

    (a) David, 2-40 (2-41), except perhaps 32 (33)
    (b) The Sons of Core, 41-48 (42-49)
    (c) David, 50-71 (51-72)
    (d) Asaph, 49; 72-82 (50; 73-83)
    (e) Various Authors, 83-88 (84-89); Core, 83 (84), 84 (85) 86 (87); David 85 (86); Solomon, 71 (72), but in many cases anonymous.
    (f) Anonymous, 89-150 (90-150); other than Moses, 89 (90); David, 100 (101); 102 (103); 107-109 (108-110); 137-144 (138-145)

The second stage represents three large collections:

    (a) The Davidic-Yahwistic Psalms, 2-40 (2-41)
    (b) The Elohistic Psalms, 41-82 (42-83)
    (c) Anonymous-Yahwistic Psalms, 89-150 (90-150)

Yahweh, the proper name of Israel's God, and the common noun *Elohim* (God) are used interchangeably throughout the Psalter, but use of the word *Yahweh* is greatly in excess of that of the word *Elohim*. It can be proved that in most occurrences of the word *Elohim* in Psalms 41-82 (42-83) this is not the original but was substituted for *Yahweh* out of reverence for this sacred name. Hence Psalms 41-82 (42-83) once existed as a separate collection.

The Rabbis who were contemporaneous of Jesus, as well as the more ancient teachers, saw in *Yahweh* the name of the God of justice and in *Elohim* the name of the God of mercy. The Various Authors group, 83-88 (84-89), of the first stage was not in any of the three collections of the second stage.

4

In the third stage the three aforenamed collections were put together with the Various Authors group, 83-88 (84-89), inserted between the second and third collections, and then the whole was divided into five "Books," considered as imitating the Pentateuch, the first five books of the Bible taken collectively.

The Core-Davidic Psalms, 41-71 (42-72), of the Elohistic collection were separated from the Asaph collection, 49 (50) and 72-82 (73-83), and the latter was joined to the Various Authors group, 83-88 (84-89), to form the third book.[7] The Anonymous-Yahwehistic Psalms were divided into two groups, 89-105 (90-106) and 106-150 (107-150). Psalm I is considered by many authors (not all) to have been added as an introductory Psalm when the present complete collection was made.

At the close of the second book we find the inscription: "The prayers of David the son of Jesse are ended," although the last three books contain many Psalms superscribed as Davidic. This note shows that Psalm 71 (72) once constituted the end of a certain collection of Davidic Psalms. It does not exclude the possibility of some other Davidic Psalms being incorporated in the following collections.

The division of the books can be distinguished by the doxology which closes each, Psalm 150 constituting a doxology in itself:

   I. 1-40 (1-41)
   II. 41-71 (42-72)
   III. 72-88 (73-89)
   IV. 89-105 (90-106)
   V. 106-150 (107-150)

The division into five books had already been effected when the Books of Chronicles (Paralipomena) were written, shortly before the conquest of Palestine by Alexander the Great in 331 B.C., for the first Book of Chronicles employs the same doxology as the one which ends the fourth Book of Psalms: "Blessed be the Lord, the God of Israel, through all eternity! Let the people say, Amen! Alleluia."[8]

5

Chapter II

TITLES OF THE PSALMS

Prefixed at the head of most of the Psalms are certain words and phrases which offer traditional information about the Psalm. In general, the common opinion among Catholic exegetes regarding the titles is that:

(a) They were not prefixed by the original authors of the Psalms.
(b) They were probably prefixed by the editors of the various collections.
(c) They thus go back to old tradition.
(d) Their authors were probably not inspired when they prefixed them, hence they need not be free from error.

However, because of the danger that without grave reason these time-honored parts of the Bible may be rated extra-canonical, the Biblical Commission (May 1, 1910) affirmed that

... from the agreement of the Hebrew text with the Alexandrian Greek text and with the other versions, we can rightly conclude that the titles prefixed to the Psalms in the Hebrew text are of older date than the LXX version, and that consequently they are due, if not directly to the authors of the Psalms, at least to very ancient Jewish tradition,

and that

... the aforenamed titles, witness to the Jewish tradition, cannot reasonably be called into question except where there is solid reason for doubting their genuine character.[1]

In regard to this decree, as well as the other decrees of the Biblical Commission, it is well to point out what the attitude of this Commission itself is at present, as reflected through the mind of the Secretary of this august body, regarding the binding force of these decrees taken by the Church's magesterium ever since the Encyclical *Divino Afflante Spiritu:*

We quote from a commentary on the new edition of the *Enchiridion Biblicum* in the *Benediktinische Monatschrift:*

Sacred Scripture has always been the primary source and foundation of the truths of Catholic faith and of their progress and development . . . . It (the *Enchiridion*) reflects, moreover, the fierce battle that the Church at all times has had to fight, though with varying degrees of intensity, to maintain the purity and truth of the word of God. Especially in this regard the Decrees of the Biblical Commission have great significance. However, as long as these Decrees propose views that are neither immediately or mediately connected with truths of faith and morals, it goes without saying that the scholar may pursue his Research with complete freedom and may utilize the results of his research, provided always that he defers to the supreme teaching authority of the Church. . . .

Encyclicals like "Providentissimus Deus" and "Divini Afflante Spiritu" show how she (the Church) exerts herself to promote in every way possible the solid and fruitful study of Scripture. These encyclicals present with admirable clarity the basic principles of Catholic interpretation which hold for all times and effectively close the door to subjective and arbitrary expositions. Thus they point out a way to an interpretation and use of Scripture calculated to nourish the life of souls and of the Church, as well as to utilize fully the gains made by modern research.

In a written review of this clarification the writer explains the distinction made in this commentary between decisions that are in some way connected with truths of faith and morals and those that treat questions of literary and textual criticism, in stating that this is perfectly natural: They affirm the freedom of the scholar with regard to the latter. The reviewer goes on to say,

We should not be so naive as to look for a wholesale abandonment by Catholics of the positions enunciated in the Decisions of the Biblical Commission, as a result of the latest statements of the Secretary and Under-Secretary of the Commission. If conservatism in biblical scholarship means clinging doggedly to traditional positions, however convincing the contrary evidence, it can be only stagnation. If, however, conservatism means a reluctance to forsake these positions until the evidence is in, until the atmosphere is sufficiently cleared so the scholar can see the cogency of the contrary position, then it represents a wholesome current that promotes progress in truth. This is the conservatism that the Church's magesterium expects of us.[2]

7

⊨ The titles of the Psalms can be divided into five classes: (1) The Authors; (2) The type of poem; (3) The type of melody or musical accompaniment; (4) Liturgical use of the Psalms; (5) The historical occasion to which its composition is attributed.

1. The Authors

We have seen that the Psalms were not all composed at one time, nor are they the work of one man, but they were written by variously inspired singers and were subsequently collected.

Psalm 89 (90) is ascribed to Moses. St. Augustine does not admit the Moses authorship but St. Jerome does. In this Psalm, one of the most excellent in the Psalter, God's eternity and omnipotence, as refuge of all generations, is compared with the brevity of man's life; the reason for punishment and death is found in the sin of man. He prays to God for wisdom and beseeches Him to reward the miseries of his life with the mercy of His kindness, that His workings may appear to them and His glory to their children.

The Mosaic authorship of this Psalm is not generally conceded among modern biblical scholars. However, certain of them do cling to tradition in this matter:

> The characteristic Mosaic tone regarding death as the wages of sin, the massive simplicity, and the entire absence of dependence on other parts of the Psalter, which separate this Psalm from almost all the others of the fourth book, are strongly favorable to the correctness of the superscription. Further, the section 7-12 is distinctly historical, and is best understood not as referring to mankind in general, but to Israel; and no period is so likely to have suggested such a strain of thought as when the penalty of sin was laid upon the people and they were condemned to find graves in the wilderness.[3]

Of the 150 Psalms, the Hebrew (Masoretic) text assigns 73 to David; the LXX, 84, and the Vulgate, 85. David, the Bible tells us, caused religious songs to be sung in the Tabernacle, thus adding to the beauty of the worship there, and for this purpose a collection of songs was requisite.[4] It is well within

8

probability that David inaugurated a new style of Hebrew poetry, the Psalm, which became a model for poets in later generations. What he had himself composed would be highly valued and faithfully treasured. As he drew upon his personal experience for the themes of his songs, so did his successors. The urge to compose would be stimulated by stirring national events. In particular the aggression of Assyria, the crisis of the Babylonian exile, and the Restoration were occasions of increased literary activity which produced numerous Psalms.

For that which pertains to the superscription *le Dāwīd* (literally, a Psalm belonging "to David"), certain modern scholars feel that this phrase meant *originally*, "Belonging to the royal collection."

The Council of Trent, in its decree of Scriptural Canon (April 8, 1546), did not speak of "150 Psalms of David," but of a collection called "The Davidical Psalter of 150 Psalms" (*Psalterium Davidicum 150 psalmorum*),[5] David being the principal author but not the only one.

A decree of the Biblical Commission (May 1, 1910)[6] decides the following points relative to David's authorship of the Psalms:

1. The terms *Psalms of David, Hymns of David*, the *Book of the Psalms of David*, the *Davidic Psalter*, which in the old collections and even in the Councils are used to designate the Old Testament Book of 150 Psalms, as also the opinion of many Fathers and Doctors who held the opinion that all the Psalms were to be attributed to David alone, are not of such force that we are to consider David as the sole author of the entire Psalter.

2. Considering the not infrequent testimonies in the Bible to David's natural skill, a skill further illumined by the special gift of the Holy Spirit for the composition of religious odes; considering too, the arrangement drawn up by him for the liturgical chanting of the Psalms; the attributions also in the Old Testament and the New, of Psalms to him, as also to the actual inscriptions ancient-affixed to the Psalms; considering, moreover, the common opinion of the Jews, and of the Fathers and Doctors of the Church, it cannot prudently be denied that David was the principal author of the odes

contained in the Psalter. On the other hand, it cannot be maintained that only a few of these odes are to be attributed to the Royal Psalmist.

3. We cannot, in particular, deny the Davidic origin of the Psalms which, in both the Old and New Testament, are expressly cited as David's, especially such as Psalm 2, *Why do the nations rage;* Psalm 15 (16), *Keep me, O God;* Psalm 17 (18), *I love you, O Lord, my strength;* Psalm 31 (32), *Happy is he whose fault is taken away;* Psalm 68 (69), *Save me, O God;* Psalm 109 (110), *The Lord said to my Lord.*[7]

From the source of eminent biblical scholarship we have the following commentary on the subject of the Davidic authorship of the Psalms:

It is certain that David did not compose all the Psalms that are attributed to him any more than Solomon is the author of Ecclesiastes, the Canticle or of Wisdom . . . . Psalm 33 (34), for example, cannot be Davidic; it is related to Proverbs (10, 27ff) and other writings . . . . Dom Calmet admits but forty-seven Davidic Psalms and assigns ninety to the Captivity or later . . . . Nothing hinders the fact that a Davidic Psalm should have been reedited or modified . . . . As for Psalm 50 (51), Dom Calmet believes it is possible to apply this to the exile in Babylon. If its Davidic origin is maintained, its final must be considered as an addition (Cf. p. 19), that which deprives it of a normal conclusion; many exegetes have underscored the close relation of the *Miserere* with the prophetic writings, especially with the Books of Isaias and Ezekiel . . . . However that may be, David remains no less the initiator of the psalmodic genre and the organizer of the liturgy of Israel. He should also be called the principal author of the Psalter (*q.v.*), that is the most notable and the most eminent. But it is unfortunately impossible to know even approximately how many Psalms have the Royal Poet for author.[8]

Two Psalms, 71 (72) and 126 (127), are attributed to Solomon, no doubt because in the former the author speaks of the glorious reign of David's successor and the latter consists of two short songs in the style of some of the Proverbs. Both Jewish and Catholic tradition attach a messianic interpretation to Psalm 71 (72). The Targum (one of the Aramaic translations of the Bible) and the Talmud render the phrase in 71 (72), 17: "May His name be *Yinnôn* as long as the sun (endures)," thus taking the Hebrew word "continues" or "endures" (*yinnôn*) as

10

one of the names of the Messiah. The language is prayerful, which supports the Psalm as an ideal to be realized in the future.

From the Catholic standpoint, some of the expressions cannot be understood of any earthly monarch except as pure hyperbole. They find their complete fulfilment only in Christ. Hence the traditional interpretation rightly treats Psalm 71 (72) as messianic in a typical or literal sense. The earthly king here is a figure of Christ the King. This is one of the Psalms not cited in the New Testament.

Eleven Psalms of lyric beauty are ascribed to the family of Core the Levites: 41-48 (42-49), 84 (85), 86 (87). The last Psalm has two inscriptions: Core and a Coreite named Heman, also of the tribe of Levi.

The Coreites are mentioned among the Levitical choristers in the Temple.[9] The title indicates a collection of songs by various authors of their family, or of their posterity,[10] or simply because it issued from a Coreite collection of unknown author.

Asaph, son of Barachias, a Levite, is stated to have written twelve Psalms: 49 (50), 72-82 (73-83). The last Psalm has also been computed to a later period, as we shall see. Asaph was a contemporary of David, famous for his skill as a musician, and one of those selected to superintend the musical arrangements when the ark was brought to Jerusalem.[11] He is mentioned elsewhere in connection with the Temple music. He probably began the compilation of a hymnal which was added to by his descendants, some of whom were famed as singers in the time of the exile.[12] Psalm 88 (89) was composed by Ethan, like Heman of the tribe of Levi.[13] Ethan, Heman and Core would seem to have names of Canaanite origin. Canaan, the chosen land for music, furnished Egypt and Assyria with artists and instruments. From the time of El Amarna (14th c.), poetry flourished in Canaan.[14]

A large number of Psalms, listed variously as 34, with a much smaller number in the LXX, 38 in the Vulgate, and 50 in the

11

Masoretic text, bear no inscription as to their origin. They are called "ownerless" in Greek texts and "orphaned" in the Talmud.

As previously stated, the question as to whether we have Psalms composed as late as the Maccabean age has come greatly to the fore in recent times. One argument against it might be that Sirach, who wrote his book *Ecclesiasticus* around 190 B.C., makes numerous allusions to all parts of the Psalms, so that the Psalter was presumedly in its present form of 150 Psalms at his time, a generation before the Maccabees. A much stronger argument is the fact that when the Septuagint Psalter was made, certainly not later than 150 B.C., the 150 Psalms had already had a long and complicated career.

Nothing obliges to report to Maccabean times the national elegies 43, 78, 82 (44, 79, 83), which are in complete accordance with the sack of Jerusalem by the Chaldeans in 586.[15] Artur Weiser holds that the existence of Maccabean Psalms, considering the distinct difference between the canonical Psalms and the literature of Qumran (Cf. p. 23) and the later Psalms of Solomon, in the time of Pompey, is, "upon the whole, improbable" (überhaupt unwahrscheinlich).[16]

The Biblical Commission (May 1, 1910) does not deny the presence of any Maccabean Psalms in the Psalter. However, in view of the difficulty of historical confirmation for this authorship, while at the same time placing no hindrance to their inspired character, the Commission will not allow that many Psalms be ascribed to the Maccabean era.[17]

2. Terms for Certain Types of Hebrew Poems

The word *shîr* (song) is used for Psalm 45 (46), and with the addition of *hammăᶜalôt* (ascents) for Psalms 119-133 (120-134). *Shîr* is closely related in meaning to the word *mizmôr*. The distinction may lie in that the *mizmôr* was *chanted* (recitative) to musical accompaniment: "Give thanks to the Lord on the

12

harp; with the ten-stringed lyre sing his praises" (Ps. 32, 2), while the *shîr* was *sung* with modulated voice: "There our captors asked of us the lyrics of our songs" (Ps. 136, 3).

The *maśkîl* (in the Greek "to make understood," in the Vulgate *intellectus*) is found in the titles of thirteen Psalms: 31 (32), 41-44 (42-45), 51-54 (52-55), etc., and in the text of Psalm 46 (47), verse 8, where the Vulgate transcribes it *sapienter* (*psallite*), "Sing ye praises wisely." From the Hebrew root *śākal* it is seen to indicate the word "skill" (*peritam, artificium*). However, the exact meaning is not determined.

The word *miktām* (rendered in Greek, "to inscribe on a stele," in the Vulgate *inscriptio*, following the LXX, from *miktāb*; others derive it from *ketem*, gold, hence *aureum carmen*, "song of gold") is prefixed to Psalms 15 (16) and 55-59 (56-60), and is also found in the Canticle of Ezechias (Is. 38, 9). It has the sense of a choice or artistic poem rather than a pious meditation. The meaning is, however, not clear.

The word *šiggayôn* is used only for Psalm 7. It is derived either from the Hebrew *šāgāh*, "to wander aimlessly, stagger" (*errare*), or from *šāgaᶜ* ("to be wild," *furore*); thus possibly similar to a dithyrambic song of impassioned character.[18]

3. The Type of Melody or Musical Accompaniment

The title *ᶜal ᶜălāmôt* ("on virgins", soprano) for Psalm 45 (46) probably indicates instruments of high soprano pitch. Some consider this as pertaining to a melody whose words start with "virgins." The title *ᶜal haššᵉmînît* ("on the eighth"), used for Psalms 6 and 11 (12), means an octave lower. Three of the Psalms, 8, 80, 83 (8, 81, 84), are superscribed "Upon the *gittît*." The Targum connects the term with the city named Gath, suggesting a musical instrument or melody which has a Philistine origin. The Midrash (Jewish exegetical treatise of the Old Testament, dating from about the fourth to the twelfth century) sees a connection with Hebrew *gath*, "a wine-press," hence possibly a tune connected with vintage songs. Three Psalms, 44, 68, 79 (45, 69, 80), carry the title *ᶜal šošannîm* ("on lilies"). This is probably a direction that the melody was to be sung to a tune so named; one Psalm, 59 (60), employs *ᶜal šûšan ᶜēdût* ("on lily of testimony"), to which the preceding Psalm is compared. The title *ᶜal mahᵃlat* ("on affliction") occurs alone for Psalm 52 (53); to it is added *lᵉ ᶜannôt* ("for oppressing") for Psalm 87 (88). These, too, are the names of melodies so-called. The title *ᶜal mût labbēn* ("on death to the son") for Psalm 9 is most likely a direction to the leader of the orchestra, indicating a song whose melody was to accompany the Psalm.

The title *ᶜal yônat 'ēlem rᵉhôqîm* ("on the dove of the terebinth of the distant ones"), used for Psalm 55 (56), is paraphrased by the Targum, "concerning the community of Israel likened to a silent dove when they are far from the cities and repent and praise the Lord of the universe."[19] The LXX and Vulgate interpret it, "For a people that is removed at a distance from the sanctuary." The title *'al tašhēt* ("do not destroy"), used for Psalms 56, 57, 58, 74 (57, 58, 59, 75), is probably not the beginning of a melody, but the memorandum of an early scribe who wanted to make sure that his copy would not get lost. A similar document is put on some Babylonian documents which were not to be destroyed but kept in the archives. Another interpretation has the term indicate an air already known or could allude to a word of David (I, Sam., 26, 9). The expression occurs again in Deuteronomy (9, 26) and Isaias (65, 8).

The ritual acclamation "Alleluia" (Praise Yahweh) is found in Hebrew at the beginning of ten and at the end of thirteen Psalms. But the Greek, in accordance with a rabbinical tradition, has put this rubric at the beginning and not at the end.

Besides the musical annotations, directions are sometimes given to certain individuals. Two Psalms, 38, 76 (39, 77), use the name of Idithun in the headings. He is mentioned several times in the Books of Chronicles (Paralipomena) as director of the Temple choir. The title means "for the leader Idithun," or "for the leader (to be sung in the style) of Idithun."

Prefixed to fifty-five Psalms is the word *lamnaṣṣēah*, "for the leader" (or choir director). This indicates that the Psalm so superscribed belonged to the head of the choir. About three-fourths of the Elohistic Psalms, 41-82 (42-83), carry this heading. Hence the maker of this particular collection used the music of the Temple choir master for his anthology. The Vulgate misunderstood it to mean "for the end" (*in finem*).

Likewise related to these musical annotations, though found not in the titles but in the body of the Psalms, seventy-one times in thirty-nine Psalms, is the word *selāh*. It is especially frequent in the Elohistic Psalms. The LXX translates the term as *diapsalma*, interlude, and the Targum, "never," at these places. The Vulgate omits the term entirely. Although the definite meaning of the word remains unknown, it was probably an indication that instrumental music was to be introduced at this point. It usually occurs at a break in the logical sequence, which could imply that it signifies an "interlude" or "pause" in the singing. The *selāh* sometimes follows verses which contain acclamations such as "Amen," "Alleluia," or "Never."

4. Liturgical Use of the Psalms

These titles are all late additions. The Masoretic text gives only the following: "For the Dedication of the Temple," for Psalm 29 (30); this could commemorate the purification of the Temple by Judas Maccabee. "For the Sabbath Day," for Psalm 91 (92). "For remembrance," which probably means "For the memorial sacrifice touching the Sabbath," for Psalms 37 (38), 69 (70). "Of thanksgiving," namely, "Thanksgiving sacrifice," for Psalm 99 (100) can probably refer to a sacrifice of the same name.

15

From a modern biblical authority we learn that

> According to the Greek and Talmud, Psalm 28 (29) was sung the last day of the Feast of Tabernacles . . . . The end of Psalm 65 (66), said by an individual in the name of the assembly, celebrates the exodus from Egypt and the new exodus from Babylon. Psalm 117 (118) is a grand liturgy with choir and response. Here also the people sing of their deliverance and restoration. This hymn, which closes the Paschal "Hallel," must have been recited for the Feast of Tabernacles (cf. v. 15) at the time of the procession to the Temple. Psalm 64 (65) and 66 (67) were said, the former after the rainy season and the latter after the harvest. All these songs are universalist, despite ulterior corrections (65, 6; 68, 29 ff.), and are manifestly inspired by the second part of Isaias. . . .

> The Psalms composed strictly in view of a liturgical act are less numerous than has sometimes been considered. It is true that later many adaptations were made . . . . For example, all the Psalms of thanksgiving did not necessarily accompany a sacrifice of the same name; all the Psalms "of the sick" do not suppose a ritual offering, and the lamentations a time of fasting and mourning. The ritual ordeal is hypothetical and the maledictions of the psalmist are in no way incantations . . . . The place of the liturgy in the Psalter originally, therefore, seems more reduced than is commonly believed at first sight.

> Most of the Psalms betray grave occupations. At an epoch when prophesy was headed for disappearance, where the priest neglected his duties, where the menace of paganism enlarged and where deceptions were multiplied, the community of the "poor" wished to react, to affirm its faith, encourage the hesitant, defend religion. Opposed to the apostates and unbelievers was a little group of lettered men, fervent for the Scriptures and guardians of tradition. These milieux of elite are expressed in our Psalms as much as the writings of wisdom, and a good number of the Psalms should have proceeded from these centers of elite.[20]

5. Historical Occasion to Which Its Composition Is Attributed

Prefixed to thirteen of the Psalms are quotations from the Books of Samuel, purporting to give the historical occasion when these inspired Davidic Psalms were written. Very few, if any, of these Psalms show a true connection with the given "occasion" of composition. For most of these Psalms it can be shown that the real connecting link between this quotation in the title and the Psalm over which it is placed is the occurrence of a certain *word* or *phrase* in both the Psalms and chapter from the Book of Samuel from which the quotation is taken. Some later editors showed ingenuity in discovering these resemblances. But this element in the title is void of all historical worth.

Chapter III

CONTENTS OF THE PSALMS

quote

The Psalms are more than beautiful literary compositions; they are essentially human documents. They reflect life in its varied aspects as it was experienced by members of the Israelite community. In particular, the hardships of existence are faithfully mirrored; the struggles of the godly to remain faithful to their ideal in the face of oppression; the disturbing doubts created in their minds by the triumph of evil-doers; the stern fight of the sinner for the victory of his better self; the conquest of despair by resolute faith in the righteousness of God.

Such experiences are not limited to one people or one age; they are recurrent and world-wide. Hence the unfading appeal of the Psalms. They echo the thought and feeling, the aspiration and yearning, of countless men and women in every era. In their matchless phrases the human soul has for tens of centuries found an outlet in its struggle from the depths to reach the heights. "To weary travelers of every condition and every period of history, the Psalms have been rivers of refreshment and wells of consolation. They alone have known no limitations to a particular age, country, or form of faith." (G. W. Pothero) To all seekers of God they remain a grateful aid in their quest.[1]

These sentiments of praise, adoration, trust, love and the faith which inspires them, give the Psalms a permanent religious value. The whole Psalter speaks of God and leads to God; it is truly *the* religious book.[2] "Of it, as of the Holy Eucharist, it can be said *Omne delectementum in se habentem.*"

From the standpoint of literary genre the Psalms may be classified under the headings of: (1) Hymns, wherein the author exhorts the just, the nations, the universe or his own soul to praise God. (2) Prayers, the most important in the Psalter. This group contains complaints, supplications, and Psalms of confidence and of thanksgiving.[3]

The greatest number of Psalms in the Psalter are those which depict the afflictions of man in this life, and in which, oppressed by calamity, sickness, suffering, old age, and persecution, he

18

has recourse to God in prayer, reminding Him of His promise to the chosen race, promising to render thanks to Him in the future, and imploring that God free him from evil. Over one third of the songs of the Psalter reveal these sentiments of the pious psalmist. In the same vein are the Psalms which portray the calamities of all the people and in which God is called upon to save them.

In this class the noblest are the Psalms which deplore moral evil, sin, beg forgiveness, implore pardon and grace, and show that the humble avowal of faults is the condition of pardon and consequently of salvation. The most excellent of these are the Seven Penitential Psalms: 6, 31, 37, 50, 101, 129, 142 (6, 32, 38, 51, 102, 130, 143).[4] Psalm 129 (130) (*De profundis*) is one of the most frequently recited Psalms in the Church, and is particularly dedicated to the faithful departed. David's *Miserere*, Psalm 50 (51), has long been the penitent's cry in both the Synagogue and the Church. "Among the outpourings of the human heart agonized by the consciousness of sin, this Psalm stands preeminent."[5] Verses 20 and 21 were appended to this Psalm some time after the destruction of the Temple by the Babylonians.[6]

A few of the Psalms are didactic or sapiential. The spiritual guides of Israel used psalmodic type for diffusing their doctrines. They teach the right path to follow, the destiny of the good and the evil in this and in the future life, how exalted is the norm of sacrifice, and what happiness they enjoy who observe the law of God.

In their "new" canticles, imitating the ancients, the psalmists propose traditional doctrine . . . . The Law is presented as supreme wisdom, ancient and classic doctrine; to disdain it is madness. It corresponds here to the moral doctrine of the Decalogue and the Prophets. In the Psalms the Law is not a formalistic code but a moral ideal . . . . Psalm 14 (15) is a little summary of moral, enumerating the conditions required for being pleasing to God: loyalty, equity, self-denial. . . .

In Psalm 18 (19) six synonyms are used for the same idea, divine law. In obeying it a great recompense awaits the just . . . . Psalm 23 (24) recalls that purity of heart attracts divine blessings . . . . In Psalm 61 (62) a sage teaches that confidence in God is worth more than strength and riches . . . . In Psalm 118 (119), lengthy effusion of the soul with the divine Master, the recompense which the soul awaits in no way appears like a material blessing; it is the life itself of the faithful one which procures for him peace and happiness, because he places his joy in serving God and obeying Him. Profound text to which other texts echo.[7]

Psalms 36, 48, 72 (37, 49, 73) are concerned with the problem of why the wicked seem to prosper, whereas the good suffer and sacrifice, but apparently in vain. The only solution to this problem comes from God Himself: The fortunes of the prosperous sinners cannot save any one from death, when, for the good there is the hope of blessed happiness hereafter in the enjoyment of God's eternal presence, while the fortune of sinners will be suddenly reversed.

The frequently recurring "I" of the Psalms seems to be only a kind of answer to the laws of the Pentateuch, which are mostly given with "thou," as, for instance, the Decalogue; for God regards His people Israel as one individual. As in the ancient theocracy, Israel, so in the messianic kingdom, the Church, the psalmist's cry is adapted both to all of God's chosen collectively and to each of His children individually, and especially to His Servant, the Messiah.

The Psalms of imprecation, such as 34, 51, 68 and 108 (35, 52, 69, 109), have ever caused surprise to some in the Christian world and perplexity to others. It is difficult to reconcile the doctrine of charity in the New Law with the psalmist's revengeful utterances in the Old Law. Nevertheless, the Church has for centuries opened her profound Tenebrae services with Psalm 68 (69): "Save me, O God, for the waters threaten my life"—which she speaks in the name of Christ.

If certain of the psalmists protest their menace, it is to repel the calumnies thrust upon them and not because of pharisaic pride. They know that God is not content with appearances, that the exterior cult is worthless if the heart is missing, and they rebel. Following the practice of the Prophets, they insist on the practice of justice and loyalty. . . .

It is David who represents the type of the "poor man." The term is repeated thirty-five times among sixty-nine in the Psalms entitled "of David" .... Father Lagrange explains the psalmist's sentiments in these words: "In the mouth of a powerful and absolute king, these perpetual complaints and groanings of the oppression of the poor by the rich, of the just by sinners, of disorder which reigns everywhere has, it is hard to say what, something peculiar which approaches the comical. In the mouth of a persecuted Israelite, fighting against the invasion of paganism favored by the great, it is the heroic protestation of faith that awaits its help from God."

Nevertheless, pessimistic accents are rare. Everywhere the suppliant speaks his absolute confidence in Yahweh, particularly in the Psalms of confidence, wherein justice, power, goodness and divine solicitude pledge happiness and security.[8]

The Psalms which treat of the messianic promises made to David and of the Messiah Himself, or of His universal reign, extol the mercy, fidelity and power of God, such as Psalms 2, 15, 21, 44, 71, 109 (2, 16, 22, 45, 72, 110).

Psalm 21 (22) is one of the most important of the messianic group. Our Lord Himself on the Cross repeated its first line: "My God, my God, why hast Thou forsaken me?" Several other verses are directly quoted, or at least alluded to, in the New Testament as pertaining to His Passion. Of no other person is this touching description of physical suffering so eminently true as it is of Jesus Christ. "It contains the entire Passion" (Tertullian) and "describes it with all the evidence of a gospel" (St. Augustine). It is cited many times in the New Testament. Hence the entire Psalm has been traditionally interpreted in the Catholic Church as referring to Christ.[9]

Psalm 109 (110) is also one of great importance among the messianic hymns. From the Jewish standpoint the Rabbis expound this Psalm as relating to Abraham and his victory over Amraphel.[10] Modern Jewish scholars generally maintain that the superscription $l^e D\bar{a}w\bar{\imath}d$ means "concerning David," (Cf. p. 9) and that he was the king or lord who was invited to sit at his right hand, conveying the thought that while God is

21

the supreme King, David, as the chosen ruler of the people, shared his authority.[11]

Because of its use in the New Testament, Psalm 109 (110) has been given a Christological interpretation, following the teaching of Our Lord and the Apostles. The Church interprets the Psalm as a glorification of the eternal generation of Christ, His Kingdom and Priesthood. In one of his discourses with the Pharisees, Our Lord retorted to their answer that Christ was the son of David, by posing another question: "How then does David in the Spirit call him Lord saying: The Lord said to my Lord: 'Sit thou at my right hand until I make thy enemies the foot-stool of my feet'? If David, therefore, called him 'Lord,' how then is he his son"? And no one could answer him a word; neither did anyone dare from that day forth to ask Him any more questions.[12]

Psalm 109 is the first of the five Psalms in the Roman Breviary for Sundays and Feast Day Vespers.

Psalm 2 accentuates the warrior aspect of the Messiah, instrument of divine anger, as Psalm 109 (110) proclaims him under the form of oracle, the divine filiation, the messianic king.[13]

Psalm 44 (45) is sometimes interpreted as a nuptual song for the betrothal of an Israelite king with a foreign princess, perhaps from Tyre. But Catholic tradition, in keeping with inspired interpretation, has understood this Psalm as referring, at least in a typical sense, to Christ and His bride, the Church. The presence of this Psalm in the Coreite collection proves that it was regarded not as a nuptual song, but as a song celebrating the alliance of Yahweh with his people, torn from paganism.[14]

Many of the Psalms are hymns of thanksgiving and praise of God, in which His majesty, wisdom and marvels of creation are magnified, in ruling the people providentially, in preserving power, in awarding equity and justice to mankind in general.

Psalm 20 (21) could be the most ancient of this group. St. Augustine applies it to Christ the King. It is recited on the Feasts of the Ascension, Exaltation of the Holy Cross, Crowning of Thorns, and Feasts of Martyrs and Confessors.

Psalm 8, an exquisite little poem, depicts the wonder of God in His works, and especially in mankind. After preceding Psalms of supplication this song comes forth striking a new note, in profound reflection of man's status in the universe as testimony of the greatness of God. The psalmist meditates on the grandeur of His creation and the place which the human creature occupies therein. From one point of view man is so insignificant in comparison with God's works that it is surprising that He deigns to give him a thought. On the other hand, he is the human lord of the earth and endowed with powers that make him a little less than divine. Both aspects are true and there is no contradiction. The dignified position which man holds in the world is proof of the incomparable majesty of his Maker.[15] In the same way does the mercy of an omnipotent God transcend the justice of His power. Psalms 17 (18), "a royal Te Deum," and 143 (144) are Psalms of "royal thanksgiving."

Psalms of pure thanksgiving are quite little represented in the Psalter. Supplication is more natural than thanksgiving, as reflected in the mind of one biblical writer. At the same time, many pieces may have disappeared with the royalty. Two Psalms of Solomon and five apochryphal Psalms conserved in Greek and Syriac, are Psalms of thanksgiving, as are the hymns of Essenes origin discovered in 1947 among the manuscripts in the cave near the Dead Sea.[16]

Psalm 103 (104) is a magnificent hymn praising God's creative wisdom and power. Filled with wonder at the glorious works of the Creator, the psalmist is consumed with admiration in contemplation of the universe: The heavens are His abode, which He stretches out like a curtain, and covers Himself with light as with a garment; He makes the clouds His chariot, and walks on the wings of the winds; He has formed and ordered the dry land and the sea, given the water of the clouds and the rivers of the earth as drink to the beasts of the fields and the birds of the air, bringing forth herbs for the cattle and vegetation for man; producing bread from the earth and wine to gladden men's hearts.

He has made the moon to mark the seasons, and the going down of the sun to mark the day; He has appointed darkness that the beasts of the forest may come forth to seek meat from Him; and when the sun arises they return to their dens, while man comes forth to his labor till dusk.

How great are the works of the Lord!: He has made all things in wisdom; the earth is filled with His creatures. So also the sea stretching wide its arms, wherein are creeping things without number, living things both small and great. There go the ships; there goes the sea monster to sport therein. All wait for Him that He may give them their food in due season. When He opens His hand and gives, all are filled with good things; when He withdraws they perish and return to their dust. When He sends forth His spirit they are created, and by Him is the face of the earth renewed.

> May the glory of the Lord endure forever;
>   may the Lord be glad in His works!
> He looks upon the earth and it trembles;
>   who touches the mountains and they smoke!
> I will sing to the Lord all my life;
>   I will sing praises to my God while I live.
> Pleasing to Him be my theme;
>   I will be glad in the Lord.
> May sinners cease from the earth,
>   and may the wicked be no more.
> Bless the Lord, O my soul! Alleluia.[17]

This Psalm (14-18) has been compared to the Egyptian hymn to Amon-Re (toward 1450).[18]

A group of fifteen Psalms, 119-133 (120-134), occurs, each bearing the title *šîr hamma ᶜᵃlôt*, "Songs of the Ascents." Various interpretations have been proposed as to the precise meaning of the word "ascents," and the special use for which these Psalms were composed. In the Mishna, the earliest part of the Talmud, the description of the ceremony of rejoicing at the place of the water-drawing on the Feast of Tabernacles tells of the Levites stationed upon the fifteen steps leading from the court of the Israelites to the court of the women, corresponding to the fifteen Songs of the Ascents in the Psalms. It was upon these that the Levites stood with their instruments and sang their songs.[19] From these references the deduction used to be drawn that the fifteen Psalms received their title from these steps, an inference that would seem to be unwarranted, because all that the Mishna implies is correspondence in the number, and the songs of the Levites may have been selected from other parts of the Psalter.

A further suggestion is that the fifteen Psalms were sung by the returning exiles after the Captivity, when they began to *go up* from Babylon into Jerusalem,[20] a sentiment to which not a few of these Psalms correspond very well. In others of them the descriptions are seen to coincide with the period of Nehemias, when the Samaritans tried to hinder the rebuilding of the Temple.[21]

No explanation has yet been found which finds in the group of Psalms a feature common to all, that accounts for the special superscription, but the most probable explanation, and the one now usually adopted, is that the fifteen songs form a collection of "Pilgrim Psalms" which were sung by the Jews as they *ascended* Mount Sion on the three festivals of the year. This is borne out by some passages in the Psalms themselves: "I have lifted my eyes toward the mountains," 120,1 (121,1), the ridge on which Mount Sion was situated; "We will go into the house of the Lord," 121,1 (122,1); "For the Lord has chosen Sion; He prefers her for his dwelling" 31,13 (32,13).

"The psalmist was filled with a deep joy at the very thought of going up to the 'House of Yahweh.' It was the joy that the traveler feels, worn out by his travels in a foreign land, or that experienced by a prisoner about to exchange the sufferings of the dungeon for the delights of home and family."[22] The Prophet too proclaims "joy of heart, as when one goeth with a pipe to come into the mountains of the Lord."[23]

The "Gradual Psalms" are all comprised in the Dominican Little Office of the Blessed Virgin: for the Little Hours, Psalms 119-130. For Compline, 131-133.

The term "Hallel" is an abbreviation of "Hallelujah" (Praise Yahweh). The Jews distinguish a triple "Hallel." The Talmud has named Psalms 112-117 (113-118) "the Hallel of Egypt," because of the mention of the exodus at the opening of Psalm 113 (114), recited during the course of the Paschal Feast, in contradiction to the "Great Hallel," which is variously applied to the "Songs of the Ascents," or more commonly to Psalm 135 (136), sometimes with Psalm 134 (135 ff.), a litany recited the morning of the Sabbath for Easter, with the preceding "Hallel." Our Lord and His Apostles sang these Psalms at the Last Supper, as a ceremony of the Paschal Feast.[24] Psalms 144-150 (145-150) are said at morning prayers.

Psalms 112 and 113 are the two concluding Psalms of Sunday Vespers and Feasts in the Roman Breviary. Psalm 116 (117), the shortest of the Psalms, is "one of the grandest" (A. F. Kirkpatrick), "a Hallelujah writ large in two verses" (W. F. Cobb).

According to Talmudic tradition, Psalms were sung by the Levites immediately after the daily libation of wine, and every Psalm was sung in three parts.[25] During the intervals the sons of Aaron blew three different blasts on the trumpet.[26] The daily Psalms are named in the order in which they were recited.

On Sunday, 23 (24); on Monday, 47 (48); on Tuesday, 81 (82); on Wednesday, 93 (94); on Thursday, 80 (81); on Friday, 92 (93), "when the earth was inhabited," on the Sabbath, 91 (92). The Vulgate superscribes in like manner for the first, second, fourth, sixth days of the week and the Sabbath. The LXX and Vulgate represent the Jews of the Diaspora.

For the Sabbath hymn the Targum gives the following title: "A Psalm and song which Adam uttered on the Sabbath day," in accordance with the tradition that it was composed by him on the first Sabbath of creation. Its association with the Sabbath was recognized in the Temple, where, as already pointed out, it was chanted by the Levites each Sabbath.

Jewish scholars have tried to discover why this Psalm was selected for the Sabbath since it has no close intrinsic connection with the day. Rashi (Rabbi Solomon ben Isaac, 1040-1105) interprets the Psalm as speaking of "the world to come which is in unending Sabbath." A Hebrew biblical scholar supplements this with added development:

> Without accepting any allusion to the hereafter, we may find in this remark the true relation of the Psalm to the Sabbath. The psalmist lived in a world where *workers of iniquity do flourish,* bringing hardship and anxiety on the righteous. How, in such circumstances, could they sing praises to God for His goodness? Their minds were beset with the perplexing problem of reconciling the facts of life with Divine Providence. On the hallowed day man's spiritual nature is heightened and fortified, and his vision rendered clearer. He then views the situation with a more optimistic outlook. The contrast between the transitory character of the material and the permanence of the spiritual is borne in upon him. His eyes are turned away from the physical world with its cares and trials to the world that is ever radiant with the glory of God. Exalted by so glorious a vision, he is able to sing His praises even before the wicked are overthrown.[27]

Psalm 143 (144) prefaces the services for the termination of the Sabbath in the Jewish liturgy. Verse 1 fits well with imminent renewal of the weekday struggle: "Who trains my hands for battle, my fingers for war."

Acrostic Psalms

A few of the Psalms are constructed on the form of an alphabetical acrostic, with divergences at certain points in some of them. This form is found in Psalms 24, 33, 36, 110, 118, 144 (25, 34, 37, 111, 119, 145), with traces in 10 (11). The acrostic construction consists of a succession of the letters of the Hebrew alphabet occurring in various positions, the beginning of every verse, every hemistich, or every couplet; in the last mentioned case the letter may occur in pairs, that is, in each couplet the two lines may begin with the same letter. In some of the Psalms one or more letters are omitted. The alphabetic construction may have been adopted in order to facilitate memorizing the Psalm.

The longest Psalm by far in the Psalter, 118 (119), is acrostic eight-fold in form; didactic in nature, it inculcates the excellence of keeping the divinely revealed law. The twenty-two strophes correspond with the number of letters in the Hebrew alphabet, each of the eight verses in every strophe beginning with the same letter. That the psalmist was acquainted with Psalm 18 (19), verses 8-10, is certain, because he adopts the key words used there: law, decrees, precepts, command, ordinances, with the addition of statutes, words and promise, and weaves them all into a "verbal fugue."

This dialogue between the soul and God, called the alphabet of divine love or the psalter of the saints, is greatly used in the liturgy, and is recited at the Little Hours of Sundays and Feasts. Verses 1-32 serve as a prayer for the agonizing.

Chapter IV

THE MUSIC OF THE TEMPLE

The first grand song in history burst forth from the heart and lips of the leader of the Chosen Race when, having crossed the Red Sea dry-shod, their pursuing enemies lay engulfed in the turbulent waters—the glorious Canticle of Moses:

> I will sing to the Lord for he is gloriously triumphant;
>> horse and chariot he has cast in the sea.
>
> My strength and my courage is in the Lord,
>> and he has been my savior.
>
> He is my God, I praise him;
>> the God of my father I extol him . . .[1]

In the seventh generation, even as early as Genesis, mention is made of the invention of musical instruments: "Ada bore Jabel. . . . His brother's name was Jubal; he was the forerunner of all who play the harp and flute."[2] There is further mention of music when Jacob returned from Mesopotamia, with Laban, his father-in-law, in pursuit. When Laban had overtaken Jacob he asked: "Why did you flee secretly and steal away from me? You did not let me know, so that I could send you off with rejoicing and song, with tambourine and lyre."[3]

Israel entered Egypt musically impotent . . . . They had the inspiration but no means of expressing it in developed musical form. The very concept of music changed under Egyptian influence. The inspiration and the spirit of the music, however, always remained Hebrew . . . . After their stay in Egypt, the Hebrews learned that music should be wedded to religious worship, and when the Israelites learned this, music definitely came into its own among the Hebrews. The greatness of the Lord, supplication and prayers of gratitude to Him, can be expressed only in the supple cadences of poetry couched in music; sacrifices, worship must be accompanied by the dance and by music, just as they were in Egypt. Music, by this association, soon even assumed a holy aspect, and we find that musicians are priests, and later on that prophets are musicians.[4]

When Moses led the children of Israel out of the bondage of Egypt, thirteen hundred years before Christ, they took with them, then, more than their freedom; they had acquired from the Egyptians a definite musical technique which grew in great proportions in the Promised Land.

At the time of the full development of the music of the Temple cult, in the reign of David and Solomon, the greater number of the instruments were of the Egyptian type. Those mentioned in the Bible may be divided into three classes: stringed and wind instruments, and instruments of percussion.

Among the stringed instruments are the *kinnôr* and *nebel*. Both are a type of harp, the former best translated by "cithara," the Greek lyre. The *kinnôr* is mentioned more frequently than the *nebel* in the Bible and is the instrument that David played so beautifully that "whenever the evil spirit of the Lord was upon Saul, David took his harp and played with his hand: and Saul was refreshed and was better, for the evil spirit departed from him."[5] One variety of harp had ten strings, *nebel ᶜāśôr*, translated in the Vulgate "ten-stringed psaltery" (Psalm 32,2; 143,9; 91,4).

The wind instruments mentioned in the Bible are the *ᶜūgāb*, a small pipe or flute; the *ḥālîl*, a big pipe or flute made of reed or wood. The *ḥăṣôṣᵉrāh*, trumpet, is a straight thin tube of metal (represented on the Arch of Titus and on Jewish coins of the latter part of the second Temple). The *šôfār*, native to the Hebrews, originally an ox or ram's horn, is mentioned frequently in the later pages of the Bible. It is still used today, sometimes in metal form, for Jewish high festivals.

The instruments of percussion included the *tôp*, tambourine or timbril, a ring of wood or metal with a skin stretched over it. It was held in the left hand and shaken in time to mark the rhythm, whilst the right hand struck the skin. Mariam played on this instrument to accompany the Canticle of Moses: "So the prophetess Mariam, Aaron's sister, took a tambourine in the hand, while all the women went out after her dancing. . . ."[6] The *ṣeṣelim*, cymbals, mentioned in Samuel, 6:5, and Psalm 150,5, were shaped from concave pieces of metal, just as they are today. The word *mᵉnaᶜanᶜîm*, mentioned in the same passage, is sometimes erroneously translated as *sistrum*. The word *mᵉnaᶜanᶜîm* is really "castanets" as the repetition of the Hebrew root *nûaᶜ* ("to shake") shows.

The word *šālîš*, which occurs only in I Samuel, 18:6, is sometimes translated as "triangle," since it is derived from the word *šālôš* (three). Actually it is a stringed instrument, with the strings stretched across a triangular form, a small harp.

The Babylonian instruments in Nabuchodonosor's "orchestra" (Dan. 3:5) consisted of the *qarnā*, horn; the *mošrôqîtā*, pipes (several "Pipes of Pan" in one instrument); the *qitrôs*, harp; the *sabbᵉkā*, trigon, a small harp; the *pᵉsantêrîn*, a type of harp; and the *sûmpōnyāh*, "bagpipe." All these names are Aramaic; the word *pᵉsantêrîn* is borrowed from the Greek *psalterion*, and the word *sûmpōnyāh* from the Greek *symphonia*.

David was the "Father of the Music of the Temple," a thousand years before Christ, as was Ambrose the "Father of the Music of the Church" some fourteen centuries later.

Under David music became identified with Jewish religious life. When the ark was brought from Cariathiarim to the house of Obededom, outside of Jerusalem, "David and all the house of Israel were making merry before the Lord with all their might, with songs and with harps and with lyres and with tambourines and with castanets and with cymbals."[7] Three months later, when David "brought away the ark of God out of the house of Obededom into the city of David with joy . . . there were with David seven choirs and calves for victims."[8]

31

After the ark was installed in the Tabernacle, David brought music and singing into the sanctuary. He appointed Levites, with Asaph as their chief,

> to minister before the ark of the Lord, and to remember his works, and to glorify, and praise the God of Israel . . . and [he appointed] Jehiel over the instruments of psaltery, and harps, and Asaph sounded with cymbals; but Banaias and Jeziel, the priests, to sound the trumpet continually before the ark of the covenant of the Lord . . . . [to praise him] and call upon his name: make known his doings among the nations. . . .

> So he left there before the ark of the covenant of the Lord, Asaph and his brethren to minister in the presence of the ark continually day by day, and in their courses . . . . And Sadoc the priest, and his brethren priests, before the tabernacle of the Lord in the high places . . . that they should offer holocausts continually, morning and evening, according to all that is written in the law of the Lord, which he commanded Israel. . . .

> And Heman and Idithun sounded the trumpet, and played on the cymbals, and all kinds of musical instruments to sing praise to God . . . . And all the people returned to their houses; and David to bless his own house.[9]

What a spectacle of glory to God! Has any Christian celebration to the Lord during nineteen centuries ever exceeded in sacrifice and praise—day and night—a cult such as this? It would seem to soar to the very portals of the New Jerusalem!

And when David was "old and full of days," he

> made Solomon his son king over Israel. And he gathered together all the princes of Israel, and the priests and Levites . . . and there were found of them thirty-eight thousand men . . . four thousand were porters: and *as many singers*, singing to the Lord with instruments he had made to sing with.[10]

At the inauguration of the Temple which David planned and Solomon built, after Solomon had

> gathered together the ancients of Israel, and all the princes of the tribes, and the heads of the families of the children of Israel to Jerusalem, to bring the ark of the covenant of the Lord out of the city of David which is Sion . . . in the solemn day of the seventh month . . . the

32

Levites took up the ark, and brought it in, together with all the furniture of the tabernacle. And King Solomon and all the assembly of Israel, and all that were gathered together before the ark sacrificed rams, and oxen without number; so great was the multitude of the victims. . . .

Now when the priests were come out of the sanctuary . . . both the Levites and the singing men, that is, both they that were under Asaph, and they that were under Heman, and they that were under Idithun, with their sons, and their brethren, clothed with fine linen, sounded with cymbals, and psalteries, and harps, standing on the east side of the altar; and with them a hundred-and-twenty priests, sounding with trumpets. So when they all sounded together, both with trumpets, and voice, and cymbals, and organs [pipes], and with divers kind of musical instruments, and lifted up their voice on high, the sound was heard afar off, so that when they began to praise the Lord and say: "Give glory to the Lord for He is good, for His mercy endureth forever," the house of God was filled with a cloud. For the glory of the Lord had filled the house of God.[11]

Where in the history of the world do we find a dedication to the House of God transcending or even equaling this for holy splendor! And until the bitter years of exile music flourished in the Temple in praise of God.

During the period of captivity it was no longer a joy for the Israelites to sing songs out of harmony with their strange surroundings:

> By the streams of Babylon
>   we sang and wept
>   when we remembered Sion,
>
> On the aspens of that land
>   we hung our harps
>
> Though there our captors asked of us
>   the lyrics of our songs;
>
> And our despoilers urged us to be joyous:
>   "Sing for us the songs of Sion!"
>
> How could we sing a song of the Lord
>   in a foreign land?[12]

33

But if the lips of the captives were stilled to the sound of song, their hearts were ever alive to it; for the melodies of Israel were never completely forgotten.

Among those who returned home after the deliverance were "the singing men: the children of Asaph, a hundred-twenty-eight."[13]

Religious fervor brought in its wake revival of David's music. When the foundations of the second Temple were laid,[14]

> the priests stood in their ornaments with trumpets: and the Levites, the sons of Asaph, with cymbals, to praise God by the hands of David king of Israel. And they sung together hymns, and praises to the Lord: because he is good, for his mercy endureth forever towards Israel. And all the people shouted with a great shout praising the Lord: because the foundations of the temple of the Lord were laid.

The "singing men" were never idle:

> At the dedication of the wall of Jerusalem they sought the Levites out of all their places, to bring them to Jerusalem, and to keep the dedication, and to rejoice with thanksgiving, and with singing, and with cymbals, and psalteries and harps. And the sons of the singing men were gathered together out of the plain country about Jerusalem, and out of the villages of Nethuphati, and from the house of Galgal, and from the countries of Geba and Azaveth; for the singing men had built themselves villages about Jerusalem. . . .

> And I [Nehemias] appointed two great choirs to give praise. And they went on the right hand upon the wall toward the dunghill gate . . . . And after them went . . . the sons of the priests with trumpets . . . with the musical instruments of David the man of God . . . . And the second choir of them that gave praise stood still at the house of God . . . . And they sacrificed on that day great sacrifices, and they rejoiced: for God had made them joyful with great joy . . . and the joy of Jerusalem was heard afar off . . . . And they kept the watch of their God, and the observance of expiation. And the singing men, and the porters, according to the commandments of David and of Solomon his son.[15]

As long as the second Temple existed David's music was kept up with joy. Although instrumental music remained a significant factor in the service, the chief part of the musical cult eventually became song. Toward the beginning of the Christian era, the instruments employed in the Temple, as stated in the Mishna, were reduced to the *nebel*, a minimum of two, maximum six; the *kinnôr*, minimum nine, maximum limitless; *şeşel*, only one; *ḥālîl*, minimum two, maximum twelve. Thus the total number of instruments actually required for the orchestra was fourteen to which two *ḥălīlîm* were added on twelve festival days during the year. Once a year, at the "Water Libation," it is reported that all the instruments, "an innumerable mass," would be employed.

Abraham Idelsohn, in his fine work, "Jewish Music,"[16] has visualized for us a musical performance at the Temple service in the last century before Christ, as depicted in the Mishna:

> The priests on duty recited the benediction, then the Ten Command-ments, then the Shema (Deut., 6: 4-9), followed by the priestly bene-diction (Num., 6: 24-26). All of these selections were taken from the Pentateuch other than the introductory benediction to each of the readings, which were composed and based on verses from the Prophets and Scriptures. The priests then proceeded to the act of the offerings.

> After they were through with the arrangement of the sacrifices, one of them sounded the *magrepha* (primitive pipe organ with a very strong tone), which was the signal for the priests to enter the Temple to prostrate themselves, whereas for the Levites that sound marked the beginning of the musical performance. Two priests took their stand at the altar immediately and started to blow the trumpets *tekia-terua-tekia* (silver trumpets blown only by priests, for signaling purposes).

> After this performance they approached Ben Azra, the cymbal player, and took their stand beside him, one on his right and the other on his left side. Whereupon, at a given sign with a flag by the superin-tendent, this Levite sounded his cymbal, and all the Levites began to sing a part of the daily Psalm. Whenever they finished a part they stopped, and the priests repeated their blowing of the trumpets and the people present prostrated themselves. The texts sung by the Levites were not Psalms alone but also portions of the Pentateuch.

> The description gives us a picture of the service and its musical rendition as conceived by laymen, without indicating whether the instruments accompanied the singers, or whether choir and orchestra worked alternately.

35

In the biblical and other accounts of Israel's history which have thus far been represented in this study, we have witnessed the tremendously vital role which music, especially song, plays in the cult which the Creator demands from His children and servants, and particularly in the house consecrated to His honor and glory. The longing for sung praise from the hearts of God's children, both of promise and redemption, is so evident in His relation with them that He seems never to have withstood its humble appeal, be the compensating miracle what it may:

For example, we have the story of Josaphat, king of Juda, who sought God's help by public fasting and prayer to be spared with his people from annihilation before the combined armies of the Ammonites, Moabites, and Syrians, who greatly outnumbered the Israelites. Just at the decisive moment a prophet arose and foretold that God would fight for His people:

> Then Josaphat, and Juda, and all the inhabitants of Jerusalem fell flat on the ground before the Lord and adored him. And they rose early in the morning . . . . And he [Josaphat] gave counsel to the people, and *appointed the singing men of the Lord,* to praise him by their companies, and *to go before the army* and with one voice to say: "Give glory to the Lord for his mercy endureth forever."
>
> *And when they began to sing praises*, the Lord turned their ambushments upon themselves, that is to say, of the children of Ammon, and of Moab, and of Mount Seir, who were come out to fight against Juda, and they were slain . . . . And when Juda came to the watchtower, that looketh toward the desert, they saw afar off all the country, for a great space, full of dead bodies and that no one was left that could escape death.[17]

By God's own command made manifest we see, then, how perilous it would have been in the religious history of Israel had music ever been relegated to a minor role in the cult. On the other hand, it is impossible to conceive of either the magnitude or the efficacy of divine observance without the inspiring and uplifting association of sung praise: "For in the days of David and Asaph from the beginning there were chief singers appointed to praise with canticles and give thanks to God."[18]

36

Nor were these "singing men" highly paid professionals who served and sang only for the amount of time for which they were remunerated. On the contrary, they were simple, God-fearing, God-inspired musicians who "served day and night," and whose only material compensation was the charity of "all Israel," who shared their bread and "gave portions to the singing men, and to the porters, day by day, and they sanctified the Levites, and the Levites sanctified the sons of Aaron."[19]

Chapter V

THE MODES OF SEMITIC MUSIC

The predominance of vocal music grew in the cult of Israel, as the natural medium for expressing prayer. There remain no descriptions of the melodies that were sung, nor is there a record of the scales and rhythm employed, such as were left by Greek philosophers and authors. The music of Israel was seemingly taught and preserved in oral tradition only, as is the custom in the Orient to the present day. The vocal music, however, the intonations of the Psalms and the Pentateuch, as well as the recitation of the prayers, was most likely transplanted into the Synagogue (the House of Assembly), an institution established long before the destruction of the second Temple. Many synagogues existed in Jerusalem, and even in the Temple court there were synagogues in which priests, Levites and laymen would worship.

Oriental music is distinguished from that of the Occident by certain outstanding characteristics. The music of the Orient is based on an element called modal form. The word "mode," a species of scale, applied to ancient music, has a particular underlying significance in the music of antiquity, be it Greek, Jewish or Christian.

The mental impression, or *ethos*, resulting from the various modes was a favorite theme with writers as far back as Plato and Aristotle. In addition to instrumentation and rhythm, *ethos* determined the use of the various modes and the manner in which they were applied. Plutarch, in speaking with insistance of *ethos*, says:

> I have in mind the action exercised by music on our sentiment. The cause of this action consists either in the determined manner in which sounds and rhythms are employed or in the simultaneous combination of these elements.[1]

A Mode in Oriental music, whether secular or religious, is composed of a number of motives, short music figures or groups of tones within a certain scale. The motives have different functions, such as beginning or concluding a melody, or combining and separating the melodic phrases contained in the course of the melody itself. Oriental music is also "ornamental," in that its tones are either short, or, if long, quiver in a tremolo, and are adorned with melodic ornaments. The rhythm is narrative, as contrasted with metric or measured rhythm. The melodies are not harmonized (as in "part-music"), but are monodic, or one-voiced. The "folk" character is pronounced and melodies are mostly sung in short phrases within a limited range. Music is transmitted orally, with no notation other than the "ear"-marks, developed so that music might be recognized. The entire theory of Oriental music is based upon these signs for musical patterns learned by ear. Oriental music is principally vocal, instrumental music never assuming more than an accompanying role.

The tonality of Oriental music is based on a quarter-tone system, which means that the scale has twenty-four steps. However, the melodies seldom transcend the range of a pentachord (a fifth), or a tetrachord (a fourth). There are sixteen Oriental Modes used throughout the Near East, among which four are the most popular.

Semitic-Oriental music embodies the above characteristics with certain distinguishing features of its own. Whether or not Jewish music at its *origin* was based on a quarter-tone system, there is not sufficient data to prove or disprove. Oriental Jews of today use the quarter-tone, while the Jews of the Occident employ the whole and half-tone system.[2]

At the present time we use principally two musical Modes in composition, the Major and Minor. As proof of the antiquity of the traditional tunes in which Scripture is chanted today in the Synagogue, it is pointed out that they have the modal form and character; they are furthermore unrhythmical, or narrative, and are based on three of the four scales referred to above. The choice of Mode is governed by the particular biblical text to which it is adapted.

A characteristic which distinguishes Jewish music from Oriental music in general, is the predominance of the *motive* in the former, that which contributes a unique *expression* to Jewish religious song. In the Bible the predominance of the motive is the most outstanding characteristic. There are rules governing the succession of motives into a musical phrase, a melodic line within a certain Mode. The Modes are characterized by rhythmical contrast of the motives. While a scale is merely a succession of intervals, a Mode, or *Steiger*, consists of a combination of traditional phrases within a given scale, in which there is opportunity for flexibility and improvisation. This *nusach*, or mould, may be defined as the customary musical vehicle of the Hebrew prayer.[3]

The Pentateuch Mode is founded on the scale *e-f-g-a + b-c-d-e*, a combination of two tetrachords. There is the same sequence of steps and half-steps in this scale as in those of the Greek Dorian and the Church Phrygian, or Third, Mode. The Mode of the Pentateuch expresses dignity and is elevating in spirit. This Mode is common in all Oriental and Italian synagogues with the exception of the Yemenite and Spanish-Oriental. Neither does it occur in the Ashkenazic communities. The Yemenites, of southern Arabia, remained quite isolated and were little touched by European customs. However, the Ashkenazic communities of eastern Europe, and notably in Lithuania, use this Mode for the Canticle of Canticles, with the difference that through German influence the Major scale was applied to the tonic and it became *c* instead of *e*. The procedure of changing the ancient Dorian scale to the Major is typical in the Ashkenazic song of the Synagogue. To the Jew this major character does not necessarily signify joy. As a matter of fact some of the most staid and the most tearful music have grown out of scales that figure the major third.

40

For the Books of Ruth and Ecclesiastes there are closely related Modes to the Pentateuch, but the motives are of a different nature. Also for the poetical portions of the Pentateuch: the Song of the Sea (Exod., 15), the Ten Commandments (Exod., 20, 2-17), and the Blessing of Moses (Deut., 33), there are special Modes employed in several communities. [4]

The Mode of the Prophets is based on the scale d-e-f-g + a-b-c-d, like the Mode of the Pentateuch based on a tetrachordal system. This scale has the same sequences of steps and half-steps as the Greek Phrygian and the Church Dorian, or First, Mode. In some instances the b is flatted. This scale then has the same sequence of steps and half-steps as the Greek Aeolian and the Church Hypodorian, or Second, Mode. This is the standard scale in Jewish music, not only in the Synagogue but in folk music as well. Nearly eighty percent of Jewish music is based on it. It expresses what the Jews call the "outpouring of the soul," so is used for the exhortations of the Prophets as well as for Lamentations and for the Psalms whose texts are of an emotional or pleading and fervent character. The Prophetic Mode seems to have been one of the chief strains in Semitic music, particularly in ancient times, for the Persian and Yemenite Jews use it for the Pentateuch also.

The Prophetic Mode has been well preserved through the obligatory singing of a portion of the Prophets—*Haftara*—the concluding portion after the reading of the Prophets. Lamentations are likewise sung in this Mode, except among the Ashkenazim. The lamentative character is expressed mainly through the melodic line, which is short and produces the effect of depression. Lamentations are sung on the 9th of Ab, in the evening and in the morning, in commemoration of the destruction of the Temple. [5]

The Mode of Job is based on the tetrachord f-g-a-b^b, an identical sequence of steps and half-steps as found in the Greek Ionian tetrachord and the Church Lydian, or Fifth, Mode tetrachord modified with b^b. Among the Oriental and Sephardic

41

(Spanish) Jews, Job is read on the 9th of Ab immediately after Lamentations.

The three Books, Job, Proverbs and Psalms, have the construction of short two-part phrases, possibly to make them suitable for public singing and response. This form shaped the form of their Modes by moulding them into two-part periods, and for the three-part verses into three-part periods. There is striking similarity between the Gregorian Chant melody of Lamentations sung at the Tenebrae service of Holy Week and the Sephardic-Oriental melody of Job. Baruch Cohon finds points of similarity in the melodic structure of the Gradual *Haec dies* and the Ashkenazic Festive Mode, that would indicate a common source.

The Psalms were sung not only in the Temple, but outside as well, throughout Palestine. As in the Synagogue, so in the Church, they constitute the basic text of liturgical prayer. In the Temple they were sung by the Levitical choir and the developed orchestra described in the previous chapter. Besides the predominantly two- and three-part form already referred to, the Psalms have other forms, in accordance with the type of feast, joyous or sad, simple or solemn, for which they were employed. This affected the Mode which was used to intone them. In addition, if a Psalm was used as an interlude between prayers sung in a certain Mode, the latter Mode was, as a rule, transferred also to the Psalm, a procedure which is called *meiyana*, in the same subject or theme. Thus any one of the three scales just described might be used for the Psalms. The Biblical Modes are of ancient age, probably preceding the destruction of the second Temple. They are the remainder of the Jewish branch of the Semitic-Oriental Song. [6]

We read in the Bible that as far back as David's time "Chonenias, chief of the Levites, presided over the prophecy, to give out the tunes, for he was very skillful." [7] Here the chronicler is alluding to sung praises of God called *prophecy*, especially because these singers were often inspired men. From the beginning, not only the Psalms were chanted or sung, but also extemporaneous prayers of praise or supplication. Of the elaborate Temple music, the Synagogue retained only the chants in the Palestine Folk Modes, which remain today for the Bible and prayers.

Esdras was the first to arrange public reading of the Pentateuch.[8] The Books of which public reading became obligatory are the Pentateuch, Prophets, Esther, Lamentations, Ruth, Ecclesiastes, Song of Songs, Psalms, and, in some communities, Job. All of these Books are now provided with tunes, whereas for the Books that were not read in public, Esdras, Nehemias (II Esdras) and Chronicles (Paralipomena), there are no tunes.

As far back as the first century there is mention of the *Trop*, *cantillation* of the Bible, a musical voice modulation which may have evolved from an expression given to word meaning, conveying to the listener the feeling for discerning long and short phrases, and cadences of line and verse, before the invention of graphic signs.[9] Saint Luke tells us (4, 16 ff.) of the occasion on which Jesus read in the Synagogue on the Sabbath. He read a text from the Prophet Isaias (61, 1 f.), as concluding portion (*Haftara*) to the reading of the Pentateuch. The reading, on which He preached, was actually a modulation, wherein He conformed to the custom of His time in observing the musical accents and punctuations, as was the custom of all Israelites who were invited to read passages from the Law and the Prophets.

The advice given to a Palestine authority not to read the Bible without *singing*, dates from the third century of our era. The reader now had to be versed not only in the text of the Scripture with all its traditional variants and musical renditions, but in all the traditional Modes as well. Knowledge of the Scripture grew to the extent that almost every member of the congregation was able to read from the Law and the Prophets. For the parts less in use, as the "five-scrolls" (*megilloth*) a scribe (*sôfēr*) was employed.

The custom developed, however, that for a part of the Law and the Prophets the congregation was called upon to chant it, while the community reader (*qôrē*) was present to help out in case the layman made a mistake. This custom lasted for centuries and is still prevalent in Yemen. This is historical proof of the wide-spread familiarity with the ancient traditional Modes, of their simplicity and of their folk character.[10] From this custom the function of the precentor developed, the post now held by the *hazzan* in the Synagogue. In our country the precentor is called the kantor. This function was carried on in the Church by the cantor.*

---

* For more developed study of this vast subject than a work of this dimension can go into, the reader is referred to Abraham Idelsohn's "Jewish Music" in the 1948 edition as well as to Baruch J. Cohon's detailed and highly illustrated article "The Structure of the Synagogue Prayer."

Chapter VI

FORM AND RHYTHM IN THE TEMPLE MUSIC AND THE PSALTER

The Dance

The dance (*māḥôl*) was considered an integral part of the religious ceremonies of Israel, but only as an interpretation of the sacred text. At the time the ark was taken from Cariathiarum and "David and all the house of Israel were making merry before the Lord," the chronicler continues the description of David's exultation as follows: "And David danced with all his might before the Lord."[1] "David sang because he was possessed of a divine message, which created on the spot, simultaneously, the words of his mouth, the notes of his lyre, and the dance of his feet."[2] Thus was the rhythm of poetry, music and the dance united. The dance is also mentioned in the Psalter: "Let them praise his name in the festive dance" (149,3); "Praise him with timbrel and dance" (150,4).

The dance fell into disuse in Jerusalem, but a procession around the altar was retained in the Temple: "Join in procession with leafy boughs up to the horns of the altar" (Ps. 117,27). On the Feast of Tabernacles the procession was accompanied with singing: "We beseech Thee, O Lord, save! We beseech Thee, O Lord, make us now to prosper!" concluding with, "Beauty to Thee, O Altar," or "To God and to Thee, O Altar!" This custom survived in the synagogues, and is still practiced on several occasions to the present day.[3]

Form

The Psalms, as we have seen, were never read, but chanted, or sung in more elaborate form. From the account of Rabbi

45

Akiba of the first decades of the second century (executed 135 A.D.), who, either as a little boy, witnessed the Temple service before its destruction in 70 A.D., or heard from some of the survivors a description of them, we learn that there were three principal forms of responsorial public singing:

(1) The leader intoned the first half-verse, whereupon the congregation repeated it. Then the leader sang each succeeding half-line, the congregation always repeating the same first half-line, which became a refrain throughout the entire song. This is the form in which the adults sang the "Hallel," and, according to Rabbi Akiba, was used also for the Song of the Sea. This form of singing the "Hallel" is still used in Southern Arabia . . . . The same form was made use of by ancient Syrians and Babylonians in laudations and supplications. [It may be assumed that Christ and the Apostles sang the "Hallel" in this manner at the Last Supper.][4]

(2) The leader sang a half-line at a time and the congregation repeated what he had last sung. It was said by Rabbi Eliazer that this was the form used to instruct the school children.

(3) The leader sang the whole first line, to which the congregation responded with the second line of the same verse, continuing in this manner to the end of the strophe. The *Shema* (Deut., 6: 4-9) was recited in public in this manner, as Rabbi Nehemiah explained, and is still used by Babylonian Jews for chanting the "Hallel" at Passover. Often other refrains were used by the people, mostly in public worship, such as *Amen, Hallelujah, Hoshiana* (O Help!), *Anenu* (Answer us!), etc.[5] Several of the Hebrew Psalms have "Hallelujah" in their heading, an invitation to the congregation to respond.

The oldest song-form in the Church is the responsorial form. The infant Church continued to use many Hebrew ejaculations as popular responses, such as *Amen, Hosanna, Alleluia,* during the liturgical services, in order to preserve unchanged certain traditional customs. At the close of the doxologies at the end of each of the Books of Psalms (Psalm 150 is one long doxology in itself), the early Christian assembly answered "Amen," following the custom of the people in the Temple. St. Athanasius, speaking of the place of the "Alleluia" in the Psalms, calls it a "refrain" or a "response."

46

Psalm 90 (91) suggests a response as alternation of the first and second person. The Targum explains the poem as a dialogue between David and Solomon. The former begins at verse 2, Solomon responds at verse 9, and God intervenes at verse 10. The Psalm may also be interpreted as the psalmist's song of praise for the benefits of trusting in God (1-13), with God Himself responding in the epilogue, confirming the psalmist's words (14-16).[7]

The last half of Psalm 113 (115) would indicate that either verses 1-8 and 16-18 were sung by the precentor with a response by the choir, or that the responses in verses 9-11 were sung by the people, in the manner of a litany, with a blessing given by the priests (12-15), followed by a short hymn of praise. Psalm 134 (135) is very similar in construction and contents to 113B (115).[8] The short three-versed Psalm 133 (134), the final one in the Gradual Psalms, contains the greetings addressed by the worshippers to the priests and Levites (1-2), who were on duty day and night, together with the responses of the latter in the form of a blessing.

Psalm 135 (136), as already stated, was often called the "Great Hallel" in the Jewish liturgy. The half-verses, probably sung by the precentor, were interspersed with the ever-recurring refrain, "for his mercy endureth forever," during the entire twenty-six verses, sung by the choir of Levites or by the congregation.

At the conclusion of the Psalms which close each of the first four of the five books of the Hebrew Psalter, "the precentor added a doxology ending with: And say ye 'Amen,' whereupon the congregation responded 'Amen, Amen,' "[9] or "Amen, Hallelujah." To each of the holy imprecations uttered by the Levites upon the transgressions of the Law, described in Deuteronomy (27: 15-26), the people responded, "Amen."

While responsorial singing is frequently mentioned in the Bible, antiphonal form, alternate singing of balanced groups, is rarely spoken of. We find an example of it in the celebration previously described at the dedication of the wall of Jerusalem during the time of Esdras and Nehemias, when "the two great choirs" sang alternately, or antiphonally, "one on the right hand of the wall . . . and the second choir of them that gave thanks . . . on the opposite side."[10] From the dialogue structure of Psalm 23 (24), it seems possible that this Psalm was composed for liturgical use. The presence of the refrain in Psalm 66 (67) and Psalm 106 (107, 4-32), could reveal the effect of alternating choirs.[11]

Both responsorial and antiphonal singing were continued in the new-born Church. We have seen that the early Christians responded in many instances with the same Hebrew ejaculations as their Jewish fore-fathers. Not only in the liturgical services, but in the exterior cult as well, responsorial singing, in particular, was practiced by the singers and the people.

Psalm 135 (136) was frequently used during the persecutions of the early Christian era. St. Athanasius instructed the congregation at Alexandria to respond to the verses sung by the deacons. On another occasion, at the translation of the relics of Saint Babylas from Daphne to Antioch, those who knew the Psalms the better sang the verses, and the people responded in concert with the refrain: "Let them all be confounded that adore graven things: and that glory in idols" (Ps. 96, 7). The doxology was sung but the "*et Filio*" was pronounced softly, so that the Arians could not hear it.

It is evident, then, that together with the Psalms and part of the Jewish ritual (a replica of which is found in the Mass of the Catechumens), the Church inherited from the Temple and the Synagogue her two principal forms of singing and the function of precentor. The new-born Church, as Saint Jerome points out, avoided innovations among her Jewish converts which might have scandalized her first faithful. Like a benevolent mother she retained certain liturgical practices which were in no way contrary to, but rather in keeping with, the spirit of the Church. "The heritage of the Synagogue in its richest elements was taken up, assimilated and transposed by the Christian liturgy." (Rev. Fr. Dalmais, O.P.)

Rhythm of the Psalms

In biblical Hebrew, rhyme is hardly ever found, and metre, a succession of long and short beats, is unknown, as opposed to classic Arabic and western literature, wherein the difference between poetry and prose is clearly defined, in that the former is contained in a frame-work of metre, and (sometimes) rhyme, while the latter is free or narrative in character. Nevertheless, an obvious distinction does exist between sections of the Scriptures which may be classified respectively as prose and poetry. It is apparent that in the construction of a Psalm and that of a historical book of Scripture, there are marked characteristics which differentiate them and which are not based on the same principles as in other languages.

In the sacred literature of Israel, lyric and didactic poetry attained a high degree of development. One often merges into the other; many of the Psalms are didactic rather than lyric, while the didactic Books of Job, for example, contain many lyric passages. Epic and dramatic poetry do not occur in Scripture.

The theory has been advanced among scholars of recent times that a system of metre forms an essential part of Hebrew poetry. To establish this theory constant textual emendations would have to be made; in other words, the Psalm would have to be adapted to fit the theory, a method of doubtful validity. In addition, it has been pointed out by scholars current in the field of biblical research, that even granted that the Masorites completely perverted the original accents of Hebrew to the extent that it is impossible to recognize the genuine metre of Hebrew poetry as it was pronounced when it was written, there is no need of correcting the Masoretic text *solely* for making it conform to a given metre throughout the whole Psalm. The

49

critically restored reading of a Psalm is closer to the general
metre of the whole poem than are the same but unrestored
parts of the Masoretic text.

Metrical rhythm was not considered of much importance by
the Hebrew poets. What was of utmost importance to them
was the balance of thought which will be portrayed in examples
to follow.

The Hebrew poet had considerable liberty in varying the
metre in one and the same poem. This rhythm consists in a
certain *fixed* number of *tonic-accented* syllables in the line, with
no regard for the number of unaccented syllables between them,
although it is rare to encounter more than three successive
unaccented syllables. The accent more often affects the end of
the Hebrew word, as in modern iambes and anapests, and the
rhythm is ascendant or anacrusic. Certain poems are prosaic,
as much for the style as for the cadence. Others offer quite an
oratorical rhythm. But in the poems strictly called elegies,
canticles, psalms, the rhythm is quite marked.

The commonest arrangement is the six-accented line, with
the *caesura* in the middle: 3 + 3. Quite common is the *qinah*
("lamentation") setting, consisting of 3 + 2. Quite rare is the
2 + 2 line.

The following are examples of 3 + 3 and of 3 + 2 metre:

Yahwéh	*mah-rabbú*	*saráy*
O Lórd,	how mány (are)	my ádversaries
rabbím	*qamím*	*°aláy*
Mány	rise úp	agáinst me. (Ps. 3,2)
torát	*Yahwéh*	*t°mimáh*
The láw of	the Lórd	(is) pérfect,
m°síbat	*náfes*	
refréshing	the sóul;	
°edút	*Yahwéh*	*ne' emanáh*
The decreé of	the Lórd	(is) trústworthy,

mahkímat   *péti*
giving wísdom to   the símple. (Ps. 18 (19), 8)

Hebrew poems possess in particular a *movement* regulated in accordance with certain laws, a systematic structure of the parts of the verse: *parallelism* in the clauses is peculiar to Semitic poets and is very distinctive. The poet is not satisfied with expressing a thought in one clause, but he expresses it again in parallel clauses. All the poetry of the Near East was based upon the parallelism of the "members" (*stichoi*).

The most celebrated student of parallelism, the English writer, Robert Lowth (1710-1787), distinguished three kinds:

(1) *Synonymous*, which repeats in equivalent terms a thought already stated.
(2) The *Antithetic*, which opposes the second member to the first.
(3) The *Synthetic*, in which the thought continues from line to line to build up a cumulative effect.

These are the most usual of the various forms which parallelism assumes. Hence a verse may consist of two equal halves, the most common form, and which, in the Roman Breviary, the asterisk, marking the pause to be made by the choir, indicates this parallelism. However, the clauses are not always complete, one clause being only imperfectly developed. A verse may also have three and occasionally more parts, especially in the didactic poems, where the thought demands a more ample development. The verses may thus be grouped into strophes of equal or unequal length, the former being the more normal form, but the latter occurring also frequently.

Egyptian poetry also contains parallelism; the lines are almost equal and often composed of binary cadences; litanies and repetitions are frequent. It is in the hymns to the sun in the epoch of El Amarna and in the writings of wisdom, indefinitely recopied, that the greatest analogy with the Psalms is found. It has also been pointed out that Egyptian and Israelite sages are often close. For example, in Psalm 33 (34), verse 13 corresponds word for word to a text of the eighteenth dynasty of Egypt, on the tomb of Ai, a nobleman.[12]

> However, the sages of Israel insert their sentences in a religious context fundamentally opposed to all polytheism, and they in no way accept, in particular, the funereal concepts of their Egyptian confrères . . . . If one admits certain contacts between Israelite psalmody and similar literature of the ancient Orient, it is certain that it never has to do with pure and simple borrowings or of servile imitation. The analogies are especially in the words, and not in the thought. By the purity and profundity of their inspiration, the Psalms prevail over all the rest; these mystical poems are inimitable dialogues between the soul and God.[13]

The following illustrations portray the various forms of parallelism most commonly expressed:

1. The Synonomous: a, aa; a, aa, aaa; a, aa, aaa, aaaa, etc.

(a) And he made darkness the cloak about him; (aa) dark misty rain clouds to be his wrap (17, 2).

(a) The heavens declare the glory of God, (aa) and the firmament proclaims his handiwork (18, 2).

(a) Happy the man to whom the Lord imputes not guilt, (aa) and in whose spirit there is no guile (31, 2).

(a) Be glad in the Lord and rejoice, you just; (aa) exult, all you upright of heart (31, 11).

(a) The Lord brings to naught the plans of nations; (aa) he foils the designs of peoples (32, 9).

(a) O my God, rescue me from the hand of the wicked, (aa) from the grasp of the criminal and the violent (70, 40).

(a) Cast me not off in my old age; (aa) as my strength fails, forsake me not (70, 9).

(a) O come let us rejoice in the Lord; (aa) let us rejoice before God our Savior (94, 1).

(a) I will sing to the Lord all my life; (aa) I will sing praises to my God while I live (103, 33).

(a) A lamp to my feet is your word, (aa) a light to my path (118, 105).

(a) O Lord, deliver me from lying lip, (aa) from treacherous tongue (119, 2).

(a) Do good, O Lord, to the good (aa) and the upright of heart (124, 4).

(a) For with the Lord there is mercy; (aa) and with him plenteous redemption (129, 7).

(a) Your kingdom is a kingdom for all ages, (aa) and your dominion endures through all generations (144, 13 a).

(a) The Lord lifts up all who are falling (aa) and raises up all that are bowed down (144, 14).

(a) Let ruin come upon them unawares, (aa) and let the snare they have set catch them; (aaa) into the pit they have dug let them fall (34, 8).

(a) Go ye into his gates with praise, (aa) into his courts with hymns: (aaa) and give glory to him (99, 4).

(a) But darkness shall not be dark to thee; (aa) and night shall be as light as day; (aaa) the darkness and the light thereof, shall be alike [to thee] (138, 12).

(a) Lord my heart is not exalted: (aa) nor are mine eyes lofty. (aaa) Neither have I walked in great matters: (aaaa) nor in things too lofty for me (130, 1).

2. Antithetic: a, b

(a) He that speaketh truth in his heart: (b) who hath not used deceit in his tongue (14, 3).

(a) In his sight the wicked is despised: (b) but he honoreth them that fear the Lord (14, 4).

(a) The great grow poor and hungry: (b) but those that seek the Lord want for no good thing (33, 11).

(a) The heaven is the Lord's: (b) but the earth he has given to the children of men (113B, 16).

(a) I hate men of divided heart, (b) but I love your law (118, 113).

(a) Though distress and anguish have come upon me, (b) your commandments are my delight (118, 143).

(a) They that sow in tears: (b) shall reap in joy (125, 5).

(a) His enemies I will clothe with shame, (b) but upon him my crown shall shine (131, 18).

(a) If I ascend into heaven, thou art there: (b) if I descend into hell, thou art present (138, 8).

(a) The Lord keeps all who love him, (b) but all the wicked he will destroy (144, 20).

(a) He hath put down the mighty from their seat: (b) and hath exalted the humble (Magnificat, 7).

(a) He hath filled the hungry with good things: (b) and the rich he hath sent empty away (*Ib.* 8).

3. Synthetic: a, á: a, á, a̋; etc.

(a) They parted my garments among them: (á) and upon my vesture they cast lots (21, 19).

(a) Far from sinners is salvation (á) because they seek not your statutes (118, 155).

(a) The Lord is faithful in all his words (á) and holy in all his works (144, 13 b).

(a) He heals the brokenhearted (á) and binds up their wounds (146, 3).

(a) He tells the number of the stars; (á) he calls each by name (146, 4).

(a) The lowly shall eat their full; (á) and they who seek the Lord shall praise him: (a̋) may your hearts be ever merry (21, 27).

(a) He whose hands are sinless, whose heart is clean, (á) who desires not what is vain, (a̋) nor swears deceitfully to his neighbor (23, 4).

(a) Who is this king of glory? (á) The Lord strong and mighty, (a̋) the Lord mighty in battle (23, 8).

(a) The Lord preserve him and give him life, (á) and make him blessed upon the earth: (a̋) and deliver him not up to the will of his enemies (40, 3).

(a) God gives a home to the forsaken; (á) he leads forth prisoners to prosperity; (a̋) only rebels remain in the parched land (67, 7).

(a) In distress you called and I rescued you; (á) Unseen, I answered you in thunder; (a̋) I tested you at the waters of Meriba (80, 8).

(a) The Lord loves those that hate evil; (á) he guards the lives of his faithful ones; (a̋) from the land of the wicked he delivers them (96, 10).

(a) They have hands but feel not; (á) they have feet but walk not; (a̋) they utter no sound from their throats (113B, 15).

(a) Our fathers in Egypt considered not your wonders; (á) They remembered not your abundant kindness; (a̋) but rebelled against the Most High at the Red Sea (105, 7).

(a) For in their mouth there is no sincerity; (á) their heart teems with treacheries, (a̋) their throat is an open grave; (a̋) they flatter with their tongue (5, 10).

(a) For in the hand of the Lord there is a cup of strong mixture, (á) and he hath poured it out from this to that: (a̋) but the dregs thereof are not emptied: (a̋) all the sinners of the earth shall drink (74, 9).

(a) If I was not humbly minded, (á) but exalted my soul: (a̋) as a child that is weaned is towards its mother, (a̋) so reward in my soul (130, 2).

(a) Who covers the heavens with clouds, (á) who provides rain for the earth; (a̋) Who makes grass sprout on the mountains (a̋) and herbs for the service of men (146, 8).

In the Psalter, this gem in the sacred heritage of jewels left to Christianity by our Jewish forebears, we have had occasion to experience something of the divine inspiration, human sentiment, and poetic beauty embodied in the contents of these spiritual hymns, the most sublime in all literature.

But it would be wrong to see in the psalmists esthetes in quest of originality; they wish only to edify, to instruct and console. They do not hesitate to take old formulas and to borrow freely from writings, even pagan, of the past. Their style, as traditional as their thought, can be called anthological; here there is a common trait with the Persian epoch.

All the religious doctrine of the Old Testament is found again in the Psalms under lyric or didactic form. The psalmist speaks only of God or to God. Their prayers and meditations are "theological" but not abstract; they testify to personal responsibilities, to profound intuitions and experiences lived in the framework of ideas received. . . .

[The Psalms form the basis of the Roman Liturgy.] If these inspired prayers hold any such place in the life of the Church, it is because they speak to us of Christ in describing the work of grace purifying and redeeming man; especially they continually announce the advent of the reign of God, judgment of the world on the last day, the salvation and triumph of the "poor," the Israel of God (Gal.: 6, 16), to whom is promised the kingdom of God.[14]

One devotee of the Psalter has declared that

"man is most godlike when he sings to God. And among those who sing to God the Hebrew psalmist stands the highest. In universality of sentiment, in keeness of conception, in rhythm of speech, in beauty of imagery, the Hebrew singer has no rivals."[15]

In the Preface of the English version of Archbishop Kenrick's edition of *The Book of Psalms*, the Archbishop of Baltimore pays this beautiful tribute to Israel's role in the establishment of God's kingdom upon earth:

> It is a remarkable token of the unity of the mystical Body of Christ, both before and since His coming, that the Catholic Church should receive from the Church of Israel its chief song of praise. The saints of old were not perfected without us; and we from them have inherited the Psalter of divine joy. Without doubt the Spirit of God, Who dwells in fulness with His Church, could have multiplied the psalmists of His true Israel. But He has been pleased to make the Psalter of the Temple the daily manual of praise and thanksgiving for the Church of all nations.

Then follows this laudation of the spirit of praise itself:

> Prayer, thanksgiving and praise make up the worship of God in the Church on Earth. In the perfect bliss of heaven, praise and thanksgiving shall be eternal. The spirit of thanksgiving and praise ought therefore have a larger part in our private devotions. It is a sacrifice most acceptable to God, and a sure token of His presence in the soul. It has this special grace: that it looks for no wages, no reward. It is the free loving joy of a heart grateful for the past, and for blessings now in our hands. Praise is the voice of grateful and generous love, lifted up in thanks, benediction and worship. To live in a spirit of praise is to live as near to heaven as earth can be. What can be more blissful than the voice of the Psalmist: "Bless the Lord, O my soul; and all that is within me bless His holy name" (102, 1)—that is, my whole living spirit, my heart, with all its trust and all its love; my conscience, with all its witness and sincerity; my will, with all its obedience and all its submission; my understanding, with all its reason; my whole being, with its full adherence to the love of God! Such also is the mind of the true disciple of Jesus; to whom the Apostle writes: "Be ye filled with the Holy Spirit, speaking to yourselves in psalms, and hymns, and canticles, singing and making melody in our hearts to the Lord; giving thanks always for all things, in the name of our Lord Jesus Christ, to God and the Father."[16]

> In the Book of Psalms, the Spirit of praise Himself has inscribed the *notes* and the *words* of thanksgiving, to be learned here, and to be continued before the Eternal Throne.

Part II

PSALMODY IN THE CHANT OF THE CHURCH

Chapter I

HOW GREGORIAN CHANT DEVELOPED

In order that a student of Gregorian Chant obtain maximum results from technical vocal exercises in practice, it is not sufficient that he work only from the standpoint of breath control, suppleness of vocal organs, proper tone production, etc.; he should from the start incorporate into this work practice of *free rhythm* exercises, basing his vocal technique on the rhythmic units of which the words and neums of Gregorian Chant are composed. So let us first go into a brief history of this phase of the subject.

Psalmody and Lessons (sacred readings) presided at the formation of Gregorian Chant: "Recitation is at the beginning and end of all genuine song, from the Psalms of the Hebrews to Gregorian Chant and from the Greeks to Wagner." (Franz Boehme)

All speech, even not sung, possesses, like chant itself, a *tenor*, or mean chord of recitation, with more or less inflections of the voice which are like punctuations of the text. These variations of tone at the different finals or intermediary cadences of the phrase are the *music of the language*, rudimentary and veiled (*cantus obscurior*, Cicero), a sort of natural modulation of which the melodic modulation is but a development, a perfecting, an unfolding.

Liturgical Plainchant developed with the Latin language. There is analogy between the phrasing of the ordinary language which constitutes free oratorical rhythm and the phrase of the recitative in the Liturgy, particularly in the Mass at its origin. It is manifest that there are the same kind of divisions and the same vocal procedures to mark these divisions. The differences exist in that in the chant there is a more sustained manner in

59

emitting the sounds. The character of these sounds is more precise from a tonal point of view. The inflections of the voice mounting and descending in singing respond to the intervals of the musical scale, which tells us the relative number of vibrations for each interval. The simple language, at the same time, is composed of varied sounds, higher and lower, but science has not told us the degree. This measure exists, however (*numeri latent*), for even in speech inflections are true or false to the ear. The ear appreciates it if science does not. (Dom Pothier) Speech, when it is strongly felt, seems to translate itself into melody.

The principles upon which the freedom of the rhythm of Latin prose in its liturgical setting reside are determined, although in no way arbitrary. Rhythm founded on the accent and division of the phrase line was the only one the old Romans knew in poetry as well as in prose. These forms of oratorical phrasing and ordinary language, to the exclusion of metric forms, entered bodily into the Liturgy. (Leon Gautier)

We know that all rhythm implies movement. However, that does not necessarily mean that all movement is rhythmic. In order to perceive rhythm in the movement of musical sound, it is necessary to distinguish orderly and proportionate *form*. Thus, to define rhythm as essentially a cinematic (Gr. *kineo*, move) principle, would be to confuse rhythm and movement. The *idea* of this movement is still something subjective which serves as a base of reality and is but an abstraction conceived by the theorist and philosopher. The real *perception* of rhythm is effected by the intermediary of the *qualities of the senses*. Nor are mere durations of sound, length and brevity, intelligible for rhythmic perception. Nothing but *variation in the quality of sound* is directly the subject of artistic ordering in the perception of rhythm in both the words of the liturgical text and in the neums woven around them. (Dom Pothier)

When Greek scholars made their way into Rome in numbers in the second century B.C., their cultural influence was strongly

felt in all the sciences and arts, particularly in the field of
oratory. The chant which naturally accompanied Greek
oratorical discourse was called *prosodia* (Gr. *pros*, to + *ode*,
song). The *accentus* (L. *ad*, to + *cano*, song) was employed as
term by the Latins, in like sense. The famous Latin orator
Cicero, of the first century B.C., describes the accent of his
time as a more *musical* tone, hence the term *syllaba tonica*
applied by the ancients and retained in modern language as the
tonic accent. The natural tonal cadence (L. *cado*, drop or fall) of
the voice on the following syllable produced the atonic (L. *a*,
away + *tonus*, tone or sound) syllable. Through a variance of
pitch, high, low or medium, among consecutive word syllables,
a voice modulation, or kind of chant, resulted, which accompanied Greek-Latin oratorical discourse.

The hand movement in keeping with the higher or lower
voice undulations has given us the term chironomy (Gr. *cheir*,
hand + *nemein*, manage), employed for the hand conducting of
free rhythm chant.

At the time of the Greco-Roman classic period, which started
about the second century B.C. and continued until toward the
fourth century, at which epoch classicists considered the
syllables of prose as quantitative, long and short, the position
of the Latin accent took a fixed place in the word. It fell on the
penult (next to last syllable) if that syllable was long: *eréctus*,
or on the antepenult (before the penult) syllable if the penult
was short: *érigo*. This is the law of three-syllable Latin words.
The accent never goes farther back than the antepenult. All
two-syllable Latin words are accented on the first syllable.

About the end of the fourth century a complete transformation took place in the Latin accent. It retained its ancient
melodic (tonic) character, but it at the same time became
strong. There was then a fusion of *tone* and *force* on the same
syllable, which gave it the name of *syllaba acuta* (acute syllable).
Latin as ordinary language lost the *quantity* of syllable for a
kind of *temperament*, wherein the duration of syllables was

equalized to approximately the same length. On words of many syllables a *secondary rhythmic accent* occurred, two syllables before or after the principle, or tonic, accent. Where two syllables occur before the secondary rhythmic accent in the same word, the latter then has a *ternary* rhythmic accent as well, two syllables before the secondary one. These subsidiary accents are more effaced than the tonic accent, the only one of its kind in any Latin word, the supplementary accents being purely rhythmic in character.

In the epoch of the transformation of the Latin accent it was therefore both *melodic* and *strong*, and it was through this element of *intensity* that the Latin accent acted as an essential element in the production of *rhythm* in modulated discourse. For at this epoch of the eclipse of the prosodic sense of long and short syllables, the phenomenon of tonal elevation on the accent became submitted uniquely to the empire of melodic pitch, leaving the quality of intensity alone to act as generator of rhythm. In the language of the Roman people a certain energy, unknown to the Greeks, accompanied the word accentuation. Already in the first century a learned rhetorician, Quintilian, speaks of the intensity manifest in the accent of the ordinary language of the people. Salomon Reinach says (*Grammaire Latine*) that the Latin of the "golden age" was admirable but factitious, the work of grammarians and lettered Greeks but never the language of the people, wherein *accent* triumphed over *quantity*. In the former manner of speech the syllables were *counted* rather than *weighed*. This is the Latin of the Gregorian epoch.

The accent of the word played a vital role in the music of antiquity as well. The note placed on the accent of the word by Greek composers, could never be surpassed by any other syllable of the same word. (A. Gevaert) In Hebrew music "the form of the phrases is preserved through all their variations, and despite their elasticity, by the consistency of the accent. . . .

These accented notes always coincide with the stressed word of the particular phrase being chanted." (B. Cohon)

When one speaks of the accented syllable of the word and the accented syllable of the neum, in liturgical plainchant, as possessing an element of intensity, it must not be inferred from this that the accent of either the word or the neum is a factor that would stand out in bold relief as something possessing an isolated life of its own. "The accent serves not only to give to the recitation more life and movement in varying the tone and force of the syllable, it has a more intimate and essential reason for being, bound to the natural laws of the language. Its purpose is to blend into a living whole the elements of the word, and, at the same time, to aid the ear to distinguish one from another the words of which discourse is composed. It reunites all the syllables of a word around one of them as around a central point. It is by virtue of this subordination that, despite the plurality of the syllables, the idea is rendered perceptible in the sound of the word. Without accent the syllables of the word are simply juxtaposed—they are not united and subordinated but by the accent." (Dom Pothier) The accent is the *spiritual* —not the material—part of a word. The Latin grammarian Diomedes of the fourth century calls it "the *soul* of a word."

To accent well one must know how to impress upon the note a movement of impulse which tends to *lift* the voice. While no artificial or conventional prolongation of the voice is permitted in liturgical plainchant, the accent, at the same time, should be accorded the enlargement which is in keeping with its nature. (*Liber usualis*, xxxvl, 1934) "The accented syllable should be left before the impulse given to the voice on the accent is exhausted. While avoiding any sliding on the note, the singer should anticipate from the beginning of the accented note the fall of the voice on the last note." (Dom Pothier)

On the other hand, the final, or thetic, syllables of Latin words, during the course of the movement, act as the place of arrival of the foregoing *arsis* and the point of departure of the next *arsis*. In this relation *arsis* (rise) implies *thesis* (drop) and *thesis* implies *arsis*, while at the same time each retains its own identity. This principle prevails to a temporary or permanent place of rest in the verbal and melodic movement. Accordingly, during the course of the movement the *thesis* is of lighter quality than that which it receives at a place of rest. Here it is deposited with a certain weight which varies according to whether it is a feminine ending, as that of a spondee (two-syllable word) or a masculine ending, as that of a dactyl (three-syllable word accented on the antepenult). In the latter case the ending is somewhat fuller than that of a feminine ending, which is always soft. When these principles are observed, a beautiful legato, or smoothness, prevails, not only between the syllables of the words, but likewise between the notes which accompany them.

The rhythm produced by elementary binary and ternary groups of varied order and phrase lengths, in both Latin discourse and liturgical chant, is called *free rhythm*, as opposed to *measured rhythm*. Free rhythm is governed by the laws of nature, not by conventional rules. The proportions between the parts of free rhythm are guided by instinct of the ear. The *movement* of free rhythm starts with the *impulse* of the *arsis* and ceases with the repose, either temporary or permanent, of the *thesis*.

In Latin prose there are never more than two consecutive unaccented syllables. All Latin words which have a distinct meaning have a tonic accent, even monosyllables. (The accents of monosyllables are not marked.) This does not mean that tonically accented monosyllables can, of themselves, be rhythmic, for rhythm requires at least two elements or factors for the existence of order and proportion. However, tonically accented syllables generally do retain their accentual or arsic quality where they form part of a rhythmic unit in combination with one or more non-accented monosyllables. Conjunctions, prepositions, and some adverbs even in two and three-syllable words have no tonic accent, in possessing no distinct meaning of their own. However, all two or three-syllable words in this category are accorded a *created rhythmic* accent in discourse, as are frequently unaccented monosyllables when used in conjunction with the tonically unaccented syllable of a word, or with one or more unaccented monosyllables to form a rhythmic unit. Rhythmic principles may even demand that a tonically accented monosyllable cede rhythmically to a tonically unaccented one when they are used in combination and where the expression of the text remains unimpaired.

In liturgical chant both the syllables of the words and each of the notes which accompany them are comparatively the same length. This principle is far from being absolute however, a mathematical or metronomic calculation. The duration of successive word syllables varies first of all through the diversity which resides in the material weight of these different syllables. For example, in the word *trans-fér-re* it requires more time to articulate the four consonants of the first syllable than is needed for the second and two-consonant syllable. Again, it requires more time to articulate the latter syllable than is needed for the third and one-consonant syllable. A short *e* in the monosyllable *ne* requires less time for emission than a long *u* in *tu*, and so on. Thus, when one speaks of successive word syllables being comparatively the same length, one can never lose sight of the *agogic* rhythmic influence to which these syllables are subject by their very nature.

In like manner musical tones possess within themselves properties which subject them to rhythmic variations through *musical* influence. Low tones vibrate slowly, calling for longer durations. High tones demand a faster vibratory movement and so are of shorter duration. All these phenomena are in the "nature of things" and as far removed from mathematical calculation as are the heavens from the earth.

In view of the strong analogy between the language and music, as described earlier in this writing, it is natural that the basic free rhythmic principles of the neums of Gregorian Chant should stem from the natural rhythm inhering in the words of the Latin language as established in the fourth century.

In modeling itself on the word, the *accent*, or *arsis*, of the neum serves as an essential *rhythmic* element in the neum, equally by virtue of its quality of *accentuation*. The quantity of intensity of the first, or arsic, note of the neum is proportioned to the dynamic quality of the word syllable which it accompanies. "The musical language and the spoken language are governed, in fact, in an identical manner by the laws of *accent*. Accentuation holds to the very essence of melody. It gives melody its meaning by determining in it the *rhythmic melodic*. In pure music as in song, a simple change of accentuation modifies at the same time the rhythmic sense and the musical meaning." (Vincent d'Indy)

"There is no melody which starts with the heavy beat." (Hugo Riemann) "All melody starts with an *anacrusis* (an arsic element) either *expressed* or *understood*." (d'Indy) In singing, the first note of a simple neum is given the same quality of natural impulse as that given to the first syllable of a Latin word in discourse; both are *arsic* in character. In a two-note neum the dynamic quality of the first note, be it higher or lower than the second note of the same neum, is sung with the same quality of *arsic impulse* as that given to the first syllable of a two-syllable word. The same principle holds good for the relation between three-syllable words and three-note neums, and so on, as we shall now see. In fact, Guido d'Arezzo calls neums "musical words."

It is assumed that the student is already versed in the traditional Roman pronunciation of Latin. If not, there are sufficient editions which contain this matter.

The following illustrations portray the basic simple and composed rhythmic units employed in free rhythm liturgical plainchant, as also their characteristic interpretation for execution of vocal practice:

Figure 1 portrays the first verbal and melodic rhythmic unit, showing the rhythmic identity between the word and the neum. A = Arsis. T = Thesis. The dynamic qualities of the successive syllables of the word, after which the two-note neum is patterned, are (1) Impulse and quick soften-

Fig. 1

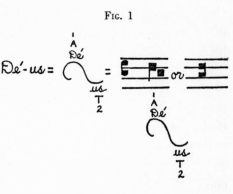

ing. (2) Weight deposited softly with the natural prolongation which occurs at the termination of successive word or melodic sound. The first and arsic syllable is pronounced with slight elevation of the voice. The second and thetic syllable is pronounced with a natural tonal cadence.

In illustrating with bodily movements that which this binary rhythm signifies, one speaks of throwing a light rubber ball upward with the right arm, starting on the left side of the body. The ball arrives at its maximum height when the impulse which generated its upward flight is exhausted. It then falls to the ground by the natural laws of gravity.

Regard Figure 1 while working out the following exercises:

1) Say the word *Déus* with arsic impulse and slightly elevated pitch of the voice on the first and tonically accented syllable *Dé*; then quickly soften *on the same syllable*, permitting the second and thetic syllable *us* to fall with a natural tonal cadence. Through strict adherence to the principles already explained, one should avoid either sliding from syllable to syllable or from note to note, or, what is equally faulty, giving

a disjunct rendition to the syllables. They should be pronounced *legato*.

2) Sing the two consecutive notes of the *clivis* on the two following tones: the first *c* and *b* above middle C. Sing the vowel "o" as in "no" for the *arsis* on *c* and the vowel "u" as in "tune" for the *thesis* on *b*. The application of these two vowels for practice is conducive to directing the breath for the particular form of the mouth cavity for production of arsic and thetic elements of beautiful tonal quality. Retain the same dynamic principles employed as when saying the word *Déus* and strive for perfect *legato*.

3) Sing the *podatus* in the same manner but reverse the order of the neums: *b-c*. Remember the *lower* note of the *podatus* is now the first and arsic portion of the neum and the higher note is the second and thetic part.

4) Sing the syllable *Dé* on the first note of the *clivis* and *us* on the second one, retaining the same arsic and thetic qualities employed as when singing the vowels *o* and *u*.

5) Do the same exercise with the *podatus*.

Fig. 2

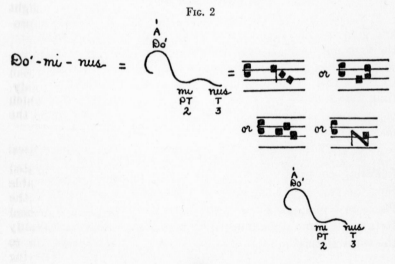

The second elementary rhythmic unit consists of a three-syllable word whose tonic accent occurs on the antepenult. The ultimate syllable is the atonic, the penult the breve syllable. Figure 2 portrays the rhythm of the three-note neums identical to that of this three-syllable word. PT = Passing Thesis. The dynamic quality of each syllable of the word and of each note of the neum, in consecutive order, is the following: 1) Impulse and quick softening. 2) Weight deposited softly. 3) Weight with the fulness of a resilient object, which, having touched the ground, slightly bounces or merely vibrates. The second, or breve, syllable unites the tonic and atonic syllables, as does the second and passing note of a *scandicus* and *climacus* unite the first and second notes of these neums.

In illustrating by means of bodily movements that which this ternary rhythm signifies, one speaks of throwing a light rubber ball upward just as described for Figure 1. The ball falls to the ground as before, but instead of its movement ceasing here, it bounces slightly or merely vibrates, then falls to its permanent place of rest. It is impossible for two *real theses*, or permanent places of rest, to follow in direct succession.

1) Say the word *Dóminus* with proper direction of the breath and give an arsic impulse and slight elevation of the voice to the first and tonically accented syllable. Soften quickly on the same syllable, permitting the second and passing thetic syllable to fall with a natural tonal cadence, but with softer quality than that given to the *thesis* in Figure 1. Retain the same pitch of the voice for the final syllable, but give it a somewhat fuller *thesis* than that of Figure 1.

2) Sing the three consecutive notes of a *climacus* on the three following consecutive tones: the first *c-b-a* above middle C. Sing the vowel *o* for the *arsis* on *c*, the vowel *u* for the passing *thesis* on *b* and again the vowel *u* for the *thesis* proper on *a*. Retain the same dynamic qualities as employed when saying the word *Dóminus*.

3) Sing the three consecutive notes of the *scandicus* in like manner, but reverse the melodic order: *a-b-c*. Again observe that the place of the *arsis* is not determined by the pitch of the note but by its position in the neum.

4) Sing the *torculus* in like manner on *b-c-a*.

5) Do the same with the *porrectus* on *b-g-a*.

6) Sing the consecutive syllables of *Dóminus* on the consecutive notes of each of the four neums, retaining the same arsic and thetic qualities as employed when singing the vowels on *o* and *u*.

FIG. 3

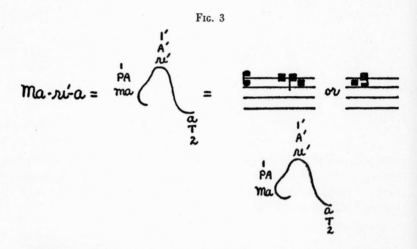

The third elementary unit consists of a three-syllable word whose antepenult serves as *preparatory arsis* for the penult, place of the tonic accent. Because of this preparation the penult receives a somewhat stronger *arsis* than that given to the tonic accents of the two verbal units already studied. The ultimate syllable of the word is atonic. The rhythm of the three-note *pressus* is identical to the rhythm of this verbal unit. In the *pressus* the first of the two notes of like pitch serves as melodic preparation for the second note, which, because of this preparation receives a somewhat stronger *arsis* than that given to the simple neums already described. PA = Preparatory Arsis. A′ = Augmented Arsis. The dynamic quality of each syllable of the word and of each note of the neum, indicating their successive positions by numbers, is the following: 1) Light impulse as though starting to blow lightly into a balloon. 1′) Augmented impulse of the same breath without a break. 2) Weight deposited softly. When numerals are uttered in delineating the chironomy, the monosyllable "high" is employed for 1′, to point out the distinction between this syllable and the preparatory syllable which is called "one."

In illustrating by means of bodily movements that which this rhythm signifies, still retaining the approach employed for the rhythmic units already described, one speaks of holding a light rubber ball in his right hand while making a light upward movement which curves slightly to the right, after which the ball is released with a vigorous upward fling. The impulse which motivated this upward movement having been exhausted, the ball falls of its own weight, as already described for previous figures. The principle of an *augmented arsis* is demonstrated in the preparatory movement made by a tennis player with his racket or by a ball player with his bat when either of them makes an initial curve behind his back before striking the ball which he is serving or batting.

1) Say the word *Maria* with proper pronunciation and direction of the breath, giving only a slight vocal impulse to the first syllable. Augment the impulse on the second syllable with a slightly more elevated pitch of the voice than that given to the tonic accents of the verbal units already studied, then let the final syllable fall with a natural tonal cadence of the voice.

2) Sing the three consecutive notes of the *pressus* on the three following tones: the first *c* above middle C (repeat) and *b*. Sing the vowel *o* for the preparatory *arsis* on *c*, retain the same vowel

71

for the *augmented arsis*, still on *c*, then sing the vowel *u* for the *thesis* on *b*. Apply the same dynamic qualities as employed when saying the word *Maria*.

3) Reverse the melody: *b-b-c*, using the same vowels.

4) Sing the consecutive syllables of the word *Maria* on the consecutive notes of the *pressus c-c-b*, then do the same in reverse order: *b-b-c*. Conserve the same arsic and thetic qualities as employed when singing the pure vowels.

Fig. 4

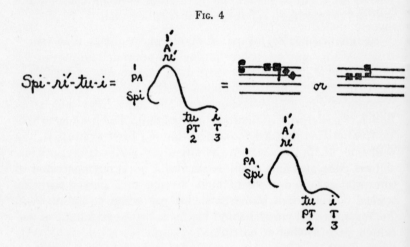

Rhythmic principles portrayed in Figures 3 and 2 combined furnish the chironomic symbol proper for the fourth verbal rhythmic unit, a four-syllable word whose tonic accent occurs on the antepenult. The rhythm of the four-note *pressus* is identical to the rhythm of this verbal unit.

In Figure 4, 1 and 1′ are the same as 1 and 1′ of Figure 3, while 2 and 3 are the same as 2 and 3 of Figure 2.

1) Say the word *Spiritui* with proper pronunciation and direction of the breath, and observe the dynamic qualities described for Figures 3 and 2 for identical parts.

72

2) Sing the four consecutive notes of the *pressus* on each of the following tones: the first *c* above middle C (repeat), *b* and *a*. The note *b* serves as a passing tone between *c* and *a*. Sing the vowel *o* for the preparatory *arsis* on *c*, retain the same vowel for the *augmented arsis*, likewise on *c*. Sing the vowel *u* for the passing *thesis* on *b* and again for the *thesis* proper on *a*.

3) Reverse the melodic order: *a-a-b-c*, using the same order of the vowels as in 2.

4) Sing the consecutive syllables of the word *Spirítui* on the consecutive notes of the *pressus c-c-b-a*, then on the *pressus* in reverse melodic order: *a-a-b-c*. Conserve the same arsic and thetic qualities as employed when singing the pure vowels.

There remains one more elementary unit encountered in free rhythm, namely the juxtaposition, or direct succession, of two tonic accents in two consecutive words of the verbal text, in which case it is obvious that the first word must be a mono-syllable. The direct sequence of two melodic accents can also occur in the melodic text.

Two consecutive tonic accents occur in discourse when a tonically accented monosyllable is directly followed by the tonically accented syllable of a new word, as in *Réx mágnus, Tú sólus*, etc. Since the tonic accent of a monosyllable is re-tained, except when it cedes for rhythmic purposes, as already pointed out, it demands a *real arsis*, not a *preparatory arsis*, as described in Figure 3. Now it is as impossible for two *real arses* to follow in direct succession as it would be for a ball thrown into the air to take on a renewed upward flight without some exterior intervention that would motivate a new impulse given to the ball. Accordingly, when the arsic impulse given to the tonically accented monosyllable is exhausted, the tone diminish-es with a slight *thesis* before a new arsic impulse is given to the tonically accented first syllable of the following word.

The rhythm of Figure 5 is also that of the *salicus*, wherein two *real melodic* (note) accents follow in direct succession, on the second one of which one springs (L. *salire,* leap or spring). For the same reason just explained regarding the direct succession of two tonic accents, a slight *thesis* must likewise be given to the first note of the *salicus* before a new *arsis* can be given to the following note. Figure 5 illustrates the identical rhythm of this neum to the words. T° = Diminished Thesis. Although the tonic accents of monosyllables are not marked, they are indicated here for greater clarity.

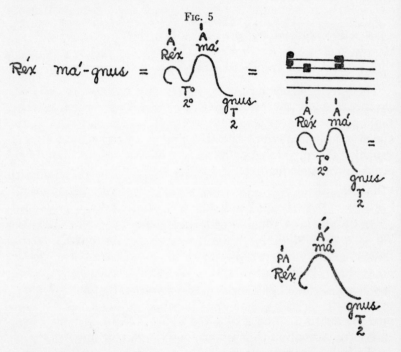

Fig. 5

The dynamic quality of each syllable or note, indicating their successive position by numbers, is the following: 1) Impulse. 2°) Weight deposited softly but of short duration. 1) Renewed and more vital impulse. 2) Weight deposited softly. When numerals are used in delineating the chironomy, the monosyllable "droop" is used for 2°, in order to point out the distinction between this *thesis* and the one which occurs in the following word.

In illustrating with bodily movements that which this rhythm signifies, still retaining the approach employed for the previously studied elementary rhythmic units, one speaks of throwing a light rubber ball upward as in Figure 1. The impulse which generated the upward flight having been exhausted, the ball starts to fall of its own weight, but after having descended very little, it is caught in mid-air by the hand that governs its movements and thrown upward again with more vital impulse, after which it falls to its place of permanent rest. This renewed vitality of the second impulse results in a more pronounced *arsis* at this place than at that of the first *arsis*.

1) Say the word *Réx* with arsic impulse but with slightly less elevated tone than that given to the arsic syllables of the previously studied verbal units. Soften rapidly on the vowel *e* of *Réx*; pronounce the *x* softly, retaining the same vocal pitch. With renewed impulse and slightly more elevated pitch of the voice say the syllable *má*, then let the syllable *gnus* fall with the natural tonal cadence and weight proper to the *thesis*. In principle the monosyllable *Réx* is not noticeably prolonged. The softening on the *arsis* should be done so rapidly that the *arsis* with its diminished *thesis* consumes little more than the amount of time employed for uttering an ordinary tonic syllable.

2) Sing each of the three consecutive notes of the *salicus* on each of the three following tones: the first *a-b-c* above middle C. Sing the vowel *o* for the *arsis* and *u* for the *thesis* on the same note, *a*. This requires special practice for voice flexibility. Sing *o* for the second and more vital *arsis* on *b* and *u* for the *thesis* on *c*, retaining the same vocal qualities as employed when saying the words *Réx mágnus*.

3) Sing the consecutive syllables of *Réx mágnus* on the consecutive notes of the *salicus a-b-c*, conserving the same arsic and thetic qualities as employed when singing the pure vowels. A *salicus* occurs on but one syllable. It has been adapted to

75

two words in the illustration in order to demonstrate the prose rhythm to which its rhythm is identical.

If the expressive sentiment of the text does not demand that a tonically accented monosyllable be asserted, it can be employed rhythmically as a *preparatory arsis* or as a *thesis*.

The principles of Figure 5 obtain also when the tonic, secondary or created accent of a word accompanied by but one note is immediately followed by a two-or-more-note neum on a new syllable. Since, as already explained, two *real arses* cannot follow in direct succession, it is necessary that the first *arsis*, that of the word, have a *diminished thesis* before the second *arsis*, that of the first note of the neum, can be effected. In this case the first *arsis*, that of the word, is more important than that of the two-note neum, as portrayed in Figure 6. Had the first note of the neum been even higher than the *punctum* that accompanies the tonic syllable, the verbal *arsis* would still be the more important, for, as already stressed, the inherent quality of the word must first be respected before the melody can assert itself with greater prominence. However, had the first syllable of the word *Sánctus* been accompanied by a neum of two or more notes, there would have been no occasion for a *diminished*

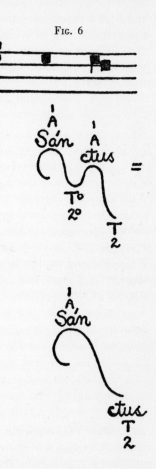

Fig. 6

more notes, there would have been no occasion for a *diminished thesis* at this place, because the thetic note or notes of the neum would have provided the necessary *thesis* to the tonic accent itself before the new *arsis* appeared on the following syllable.

For practice of the rhythmic principles portrayed in Figure 6, follow the principles explained in Figure 5, reversing the relative importance of the two *arses*. For melodic practice, sing the first *b* above middle C on the *punctum* which accompanies the syllable *Sán* with its *arsis* and diminished *thesis*, and *b-a* on the *clivis* which accompanies the syllable *ctus*. The neum accent which accompanies the syllable *ctus* is almost imperceptible, merely sufficient to properly enunciate the consonant *c*.

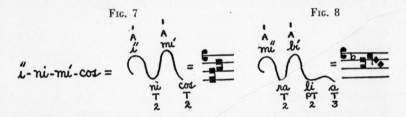

Fig. 7   Fig. 8

We have seen (p. 62) that by the time of the great epoch of Gregorian Chant production in the fourth and fifth centuries, a secondary rhythmic accent had appeared in polysyllabic words, and that this accent was placed either two syllables before or two syllables after the tonic accent of the word. A word wherein the secondary accent precedes the tonic accent, receives the rhythmic treatment which serves as pattern for a composite neum, as portrayed in Figures 7 and 8.

Fig. 9

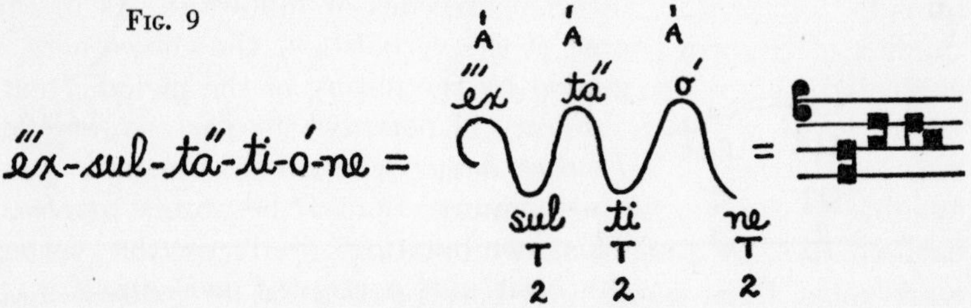

77

A six-syllable word whose tonic accent occurs on the penult receives a ternary accent as well as a secondary one, as portrayed in Figure 9. The composite neum illustrated is of identical rhythm.

We know that neither a monosyllable nor a single note can, of itself, be rhythmic, since rhythm means proportion, which in turn claims at least two elements or factors in order that a comparative relation exist. For which reason, *during the course of the movement,* a monosyllable, be it one of tonic accent or not, must, in discourse, be united rhythmically either to one or more monosyllables which directly precede or follow it, or else to a rhythmic unit which directly precedes or follows it. The choice of direction is largely determined by the sense of the verbal text. For example, in the phrase *Dóminus de Sion,* it is obvious that the preposition *de* pertains to *Sion,* not to *Dóminus.* Accordingly, Figure 10 illustrates the same rhythmic verbal unit as that of Figure 3.

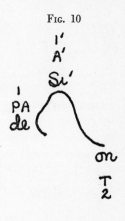

Fig. 10

During the course of the movement a single note must likewise be united rhythmically to another single note or notes which directly precede or follow it, or to a neum of two or more notes which directly precedes or follows it. As in the case of the verbal text, the choice here is guided by the nature of the melodic text.

Figure 11 portrays the part sentence of *Déus est bónus,* wherein the meaning obviously requires that *est* be united to *Déus.* This combination produces the verbal rhythmic unit portrayed in Figure 2.

Fig. 11

We repeat what has already been said (p. 64), that there can be no more than two consecutive unaccented syllables in prose. However, two consecutive unaccented syllables can be followed by a *preparatory arsic* syllable, as in *génuit María*. This is illustrated by combining Figure 2 with Figure 3, making a distinction of importance between the two *arses*.

FIG. 12

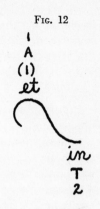

Now even when but two consecutive unaccented monosyllables occur at the *beginning* of a phrase, the first one must receive a *created rhythmic* accent, for we know that *all* movement, be it verbal or melodic, must commence with an *arsic* element. Hence Figure 12 is like Figure 1.

FIG. 13

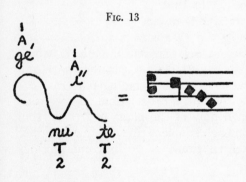

Figure 13 portrays a secondary accent which occurs two syllables *after* the tonic accent of the word to which the monosyllable *te* is united. The secondary accented syllable and the monosyllable *te* are united to form a binary rhythmic unit. Here we have an instance of a tonically accented monosyllable ceding rhythmically to a secondary verbal accent. It has already been said (p. 76) that these tonically accented monosyllables can be treated thetically where the melodic or verbal text demands this. A monosyllable before a *pause* (not necessarily at the mediation of psalmody) must always be treated thetically, be it a tonically accented one or not.

As already stressed, the sense of the phrase will determine these things. For example, in the sentence *Beátus vir qui tímet Dóminum*, the tonically accented noun *vir* is united rhythmically to *Beátus* and is used thetically, while the pronoun *qui* cedes its normally tonic accent to become a *preparatory arsis* to *tímet*.

Figure 14 portrays two consecutive unaccented syllables, the first of which, the monosyllable *de*, receives a created rhythmic accent and is arsic to the otherwise preparatory arsic syllable of the word *Aegypto*. The syllable *Ae* is now employed thetically, a principle which has already been explained (Cf. pp. 65, 78). This combination produces the rhythm of the composite word of Figure 7.

Fig. 14

In the rhythm of prose as in that of melody, no syllable or note stands out in "mid-air". Like the threads of a Flemish tapestry or the tiny stones of a Byzantine mosaic, in which each thread and each stone has its definite place as part of a small pattern, which together with surrounding patterns produces a magnificent whole through inter-relation, so does each syllable of the word or each note of the neum in free rhythm find a determinate place in each smallest rhythm, and together with its surrounding sister rhythms merge into one glorious rhythmic ensemble.

It should now be clear that the verbal text of Gregorian Chant *guides* the rhythm of the melody without, however, *dominating* it. The rhythm of neums in both their simple and composite forms is patterned after the rhythm of words in both their simple and composite forms. We have also seen that a tonically accented monosyllable may cede to a subsidiary verbal accent when the nature of the melody calls for this, all in preserving the primacy of the words. However, the condition illustrated in Figure 13 would normally prevail only in metric or psalmodic chant, as we shall see.

In a letter of July 10, 1912, to Archbishop Dubois of Bruges (at the time), St. Pius X wrote the following: "The question of the pronunciation of Gregorian Chant is closely bound up with the restoration of Gregorian Chant, the constant subject of Our thoughts and recommendations from the beginning of Our pontificate. *The accent and pronunciation of Latin had great influence on the melodic and rhythmic formation of the Gregorian phrase,* and consequently it is necessary that these melodies be rendered in the same manner in which they were artistically conceived at their very beginning. Finally, the spread of the Roman pronunciation will have the further advantage of consolidating the work of liturgical unity. . . . This is what We desire, that the movement of the return to the Roman pronunciation of Latin should continue with the same zeal and consoling success that has marked its progress hitherto."

Chapter II

ROMAN PSALMODY

The original melody of the Church was nothing other than a recitative on a reciting tone (*chorda*) with musical elevation of the voice on the accented syllable of the last word of the psalm verse, followed by a tonal cadence, or drop, to the final. In simple psalmodic Ambrosian Chant the mediant cadence and intonation are lacking. The Psalm Tone starts on the dominant and goes straight through to the final cadence; the dominant is likewise variable. In the Gregorian revision an intonation up to the dominant is added, the verse is divided into two parts by a mediant cadence and the dominant is fixed.

In the music of the Church, as in Jewish music, the two-part form of the Psalm verse shaped the form of psalmody by moulding two-part verses into two-part melodic structures. Where the verse in Roman psalmody is three-part in structure, the first two parts are divided by a drop of the voice to a lower tone, hence the term *flex* is applied to this cadence.

The Eight Church Modes

No.	Name	Character		Final	Dominant
I	Dorian	Authentic	D 1 E ½ F 1 G 1 a 1 b ½ c 1 d	D	a
II	Hypodorian	Plagal	A 1 B ½ C 1 D 1 E ½ F 1 G 1 a	D	F
III	Phrygian	Authentic	E ½ F 1 G 1 a 1 b ½ c 1 d 1 e	E	c
IV	Hypophrygian	Plagal	B ½ C 1 D 1 E ½ F 1 G 1 a 1 b	E	a
V	Lydian	Authentic	F 1 G 1 a 1 b ½ c 1 d 1 e ½ f	F	c
VI	Hypolydian	Plagal	C 1 D 1 E ½ F 1 G 1 a 1 b ½ c	F	a
VII	Mixolydian	Authentic	G 1 a 1 b ½ c 1 d 1 e ½ f 1 g	G	d
VIII	Hypomixolydian	Plagal	D 1 E ½ F 1 G 1 a 1 b ½ c 1 d	G	c

82

The Eight Psalm Tones, completely revised by medieval theorists, correspond to the Eight Modes. Each Tone has the same Dominant as the numerically corresponding Mode, but the Finals of the Tones vary in order to lead smoothly into the particular Antiphon which follows the last verse of the Psalm. Tones I, III, IV, VII, and VIII have several final formulas, varying in number. Tones II, V and VI have but one ending. Each Tone has but one Mediant Cadence, other than Tone VI, which, since the sixteenth century, has made use of two mediant formulas. Where a mediant cadence closes on a Hebrew word or a monosyllable the "broken" or unfinished cadence may be used. All of the verses of the same Psalm are sung on one fixed melody.

The Peregrinus (strange) Tone is irregular: hybrid. It has two Dominants. Up to the Mediant it uses *a*, but for the last half of the formula it drops to G. The Peregrinus, or at least the Mediant Cadence, seems to have originated in the time of Aurelian of Roémé (c. 850), but the theorists were not enamoured of it. Pseudo-Hucbald, an undetermined theorist of the tenth century, calls it *tonus novissimus*. Later it was generally called Peregrinus. This Tone is used for Psalm 113, the fifth in the Roman Sunday Vespers.

The lowering of b to b♭, both in the melodies and Psalm Tones, resulted from three causes:

1. In order to avoid a tritone (three consecutive whole steps): F│G│*a*│*b* in melodic passages.

2. Through retention of the fixed formula of Guido's overlapping hexachords (1-1-½-1-1), the first one of which starts on G. In order that the same sequence of steps and half-steps be retained in the third hexachord, which starts of F, it is necessary to lower *b* to *b*♭.

3. Through transposition of the Plagal Modes a fourth higher. For example, the Hypodorian Mode transposed from A-*a* to D-*d*, requires a b♭ in the transposed version in order to retain a sequence of steps and half-steps identical to those in the original scale.

The note *b* then had two aspects, natural or flat. It accordingly became known as the "changeable note," and because of its indeterminate character, the Modes which used *b* for Dominant shifted the latter to *c*, as Modes III and VIII. This change came about in the tenth or eleventh centuries and is the broadest modal change ever brought to liturgical melodies. However, this change has never been carried out completely, for there are still many traces of *b* as Dominant, for example Gloria XIV and Kyrie XVI.

The factor of *expression*, characteristic of responsorial and antiphonal chant, resulting from greater or lesser importance of the verbal or musical text throughout the course of the piece, is absent in psalmodic chant. In liturgical chant other than psalmody and hymnody, the original melody which accompanies the verbal text is composed around the *words*. But again we repeat, while the verbal text *guides* the musical text, there are dynamic concessions on the part of each in the interest of the sentiment and expression—artistic interpretation—of the whole.

The construction of psalmody is a very particular one. Here we have but one fixed melodic pattern for the different verses of the same Psalm. At the same time, the rhythm of the melody in its arsic and thetic movement is governed by the rhythm of the words, as in all liturgical chant, even to note adjustments being made at certain cadences in order to conform to the accents of the words. On the other hand, these melodic adjustments at the cadences in no way alter the melody as such. They consist generally of nothing other than anticipation or repetition of the same note. At the same time, *determined melodic accents* are chosen to accompany the verbal ones, regardless of word importance. It is in these particular cases that lesser verbal accents must be conformed to musical accents and not vice-versa, as is general in chant other than psalmody and metric hymnody.

It is because of this particular melodic construction in psalmody that we see tonically accented monosyllables ceding dynamically to secondary, ternary, and even created verbal accents in cases such as the following: (*génu*) *í te,* (*laetábi*) *túr rex,* (*tríbuláti*) *üm me, dé te,* etc. This is a condition which would not reasonably be met with in other than psalmody and hymnody, the latter of metric construction, as just stated.

A further characteristic of psalmody which differentiates its interpretation from chant pieces in general, in addition to the repeated melodic pattern for each verse of the Psalm, resides in the verbal texts, where, all in retaining their arsic and thetic nature, the consecutive accents of the words, during the course of the movement, are expressed with equal dynamic quality, regardless of accentual importance (including augmented accents), other than secondary and ternary accents, which are rendered with slightly less impulsion of the voice than that given to tonic accents. However, where these subsidiary accents are comprised in the *cadences* they receive the same prominence as tonic accents at the same places, as just explained and illustrated.

The entire rhythmic movement of psalmody is *toward the cadences,* where the final melodic accent or accents (when there are two) are sung with greater fulness than that accorded the preceding ones, although without abrupt contrast to them. The general accentuation of the psalmodic verse is, moreover, of lighter tonal quality than that employed in antiphonal and responsorial chant as a whole.

It must further be brought out that the *silence* in all music, vocal or instrumental, is an integral part of *rhythm.* Aristedes (3d century musicologist) calls the silence "a beat not filled with sound and used to complete the rhythm."

Since the rhythm of psalmody, as of all plainchant, is *free* in nature—not measured—the relative length of the sounds and silences must be governed as in all free rhythm: by *proportion—not* mathematical calculation. Consequently, the *pause* at the mediant cadence of psalmody repeats the time length of the last elementary rhythmic verbal unit which precedes the pause. For example, if the preceding rhythmic unit is *méo* or *ĭn te*, the pause would be the length of time required for uttering either of these units. The same principle holds true for the length of time required for uttering any one of the verbal units, such as *Dóminus, osténdi, Magníficat,* etc.

If a polysyllabic word precedes the pause, the latter is a repetition of the length of time required for uttering the last rhythmic unit, whether this start with a tonic, a secondary, a ternary or a created rhythmic accent: *(cŏntur) bátus est; (laetábi) tŭr rex; (trĭbuláti) ŭm me; (fúror eórum) ĭn nos.* In the third case we see the occurrence of a *ternary* accent two syllables *after* the tonic accent, since the secondary accent has already been accorded the second syllable before the tonic accent. We see as well, tonically accented monosyllables used thetically to secondary, ternary and created accents used arsically, the reasons for which have already been explained (p. 84).

There is a slight *rallentando* at the place of the final cadence of each psalm verse, in keeping with that occasioned by the termination of all movement, in this case verbal and melodic.

There is no pause at the *close* of the psalm verse, merely sufficient time for the final and slightly prolonged syllable to be deposited before starting the following verse.

Singing the Psalms

Before entering into the sung interpretation of psalmody, it is advisable, as in all types of chant, to mark the subsidiary accents in the verbal text, after which recite the verbal text of the entire psalm with its natural rhythm, enunciating distinctly not only the syllables themselves, but combining them clearly and smoothly into the various rhythmic units and their combinations, those which enter into the patterns of free rhythm in the art of both language and melody. Study the illustrations which have been presented, starting with Figure 1, as guides.

Utter the accented syllables with the slight impulse of the voice proper to words, making no distinction among them except in the case of subsidiary accents, which, as previously stated, are more effaced than tonic ones.

At the mediant and final cadences give a somewhat fuller impulse of the voice to the melodic accents (which always accompany a verbal accent), especially to the last one if there are two.

In psalmody it is especially necessary that the Latin words be united with as perfect a *legato* as possible. To aid in attaining this, keep the final vowel of each syllable open, placing the following consonant at the beginning of the following syllable. Where there are two or more consecutive consonants and it is necessary to divide them among the syllables, still think of keeping the vowel open and utter the consonant which follows on the same syllable softly and rapidly, even though distinctly. The difference between a vowel (L. *vocalis*, sounding) and a consonant (L. *con*, together + *sono*, sound) is the difference between a musical sound, regular sound waves, and noise, irregular sound waves. No one can *sing* a consonant, because there is interruption of musical sound made by the larynx.

Next sing the verbal melody of each verse on the vowels *o* and *u*, applying them to the *arses* and *theses* of the words in exactly the same manner employed in the illustrations of these various units in their simple and composite forms. Retain the identical rhythm with which the verses were recited. If the final cadence is that of a spondee, deposit it softly, as in feminine endings; if it is that of a dactyl, deposit it with a certain fulness, as in a masculine ending (Cf. p. 64). Avoid sliding from vowel to vowel, by softening on the arsic syllable before the thetic one is uttered. Let us ever keep in mind Dom Pothier's directions that the singer should anticipate from the beginning of the accented note the fall of the voice on the last note.

Finally, sing the words of the Psalm, observing all the principles previously indicated. If but one Psalm is studied in this detailed technical manner, it can be used as model for all psalmodic chant.

In summing up the general interpretation of all Gregorian Chant, of whatever style of composition it may be, it goes without saying that there are no abrupt contrasts of tonal shadings at any time. The same holds good for the agogic elements.

All the symbolic drawings in this study have been purposely exaggerated in the delineation of their height, and consequent depth, in order to engender an initial concept of the nature of elementary rhythmic units and their combinations in the art of free rhythm verbal and musical sound. No attempt has been made to fabricate artistic looking patterns as such, for their purpose is not to produce ornamental scrolls, but simply to fulfil a utilitary function, that of presenting in as lucid a manner as possible the explanations given in the text.

Sufficient has been said and repeated for all that concerns the proportions of rhythm in all its phases in the arts of time, literature and music, for the observant student to realize that the portrayed elements are "blocked in" in a manner to first determine their relative proportions, after which they are blended into a proportionate whole, as in all expressions of art.

The following illustration of Psalm 109 incorporates the various elementary verbal units and their combinations, those which have been presented in the symbolic drawings previously illustrated. With patient and thoughtful practice the student should be equipped for the proper rendition of all psalmody including the Canticles, which follow the same rhythmic principles as the Psalms.*

---

* A study of the Psalm Tones and Gregorian Modes as well as a description of the interpretation of the Antiphons and Hymns of the Office, together with that of liturgical song in general, is given in the author's previous works on the Chant: *The Spirit of Gregorian Chant*, and *The Song of the Church*. An illustrated description of the interpretation of the five pieces of the Ordinary of the Mass is given in the author's study *Gregorian Chant Analyzed and Studied*.

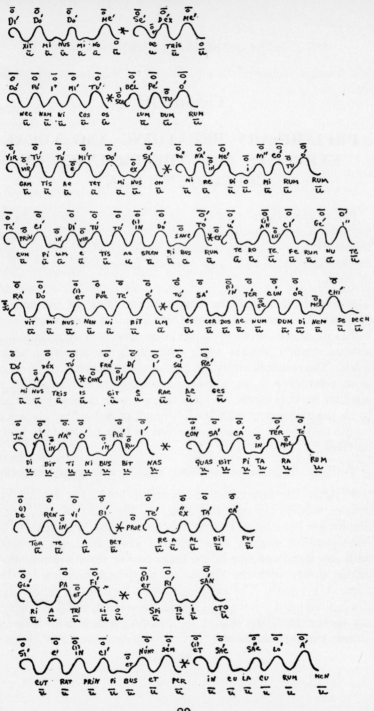

89

Chapter III

PRELIMINARY BREATHING AND VOCAL EXERCISES FOR THE PRACTICE OF GREGORIAN CHANT

Before entering into actual singing, breathing exercises should be practiced in a well-aired room. It is essential that singers inhale sufficient oxygen, otherwise their attention will not only be impaired, but their tone also will become heavy and drop in pitch.

1) Stand erect with the weight of the body on the balls of the feet and the head slightly drooped. In class work leave sufficient space between singers for free arm movement. A serious student should apply chironomy in all the practice work. (The symbolic drawings can be used as patterns.) Nothing is so conducive to one's *feeling* the rhythm as the ability to conduct it. It is advisable for a teacher who is facing the class to do the chironomy with the left hand, in order that his movements may be in the same direction as that of the class which he faces.

2) Place the palms of the hands slightly above the hip bones.

3) After the instructor has counted 1-2-3, the entire class inhales slowly through the nose, to the base of the lungs, diaphragm breathing. During this process the head rises to an erect position, slightly tilted upward when the lungs are filled with air. Retain the air in the lungs two or three seconds, then exhale slowly with the lips poised as though blowing out the flame of a candle. The exhaling should be done so gently that if a lighted candle were held before the mouth, the flame would not flicker. In actual singing the inhaling is done with alacrity, largely through the mouth, but the exhaling should be effected

90

with as much breath conservation as possible. This is one of the essentials of good singing.

4) Inhale deeply and swiftly through the nose and mouth. Hold for a second or two, then open the mouth wide by letting the lower jaw drop loosely. Raise the upper lip without tension and place the tip of the tongue against the lower teeth without pressing.

5) Direct the breath *upward* and *forward* in the mouth while singing the vowel "a" as in "father," on the note *a* (first above middle C). Retain the tone until the breath expires. Repeat the same exercise on the vowels ā-ē-ī-ō-ū.

With each vowel the form of the mouth cavity changes according to the position of the mouth and lips, which, in turn, produce different qualities of sound for each vowel. The *form* of the mouth cavity produces particular partials, or over-tones, and these modify the quality of the tone. If a scale is sung on one vowel, the pitch of the oral cavity slightly changes, or the pitch of the resonating cavity may be slightly changed for certain vowels, but the *quality* of the tone does not change on the same vowel. If time permits, repeat each of the vowels three times.

The tone should be free from either a nasal or throaty quality. At the same time, it should be *resonant*, full and free without forcing of any kind. The very nature of liturgical song would seem to call for a tonal quality of *substance* in its interpretation, in keeping with the soul that both *struggles* and *lives*—as did our Hebrew and Christian composers of these inspired words and notes—and who addresses to the Creator its highest aspirations in the language of the Church clothed in song.

The vocal exercises which follow should be practiced on the two vowels ō and ū, in the manner fully described in the foregoing explanatory material which accompanies the illustrations of the neums, and as is also portrayed in the illustrated vocal exercises. These two vowels are selected not only for their easy application to respective arsic and thetic elements, but because they are the least exigent of the vowels for a great amount of singing.

Follow the vowel practice of the simple neums with verbal application to each neum of the series. For example, sing the *podatus* and *clivis* on the word *Déus*, the three-note neums on *Dóminus*, the three-note *pressus* on *María*, the four-note *pressus* on *Spirítui*, the *salicus* on *Réx mágnus*, using any one of the eight modal scales. Respect rhythmic and tonal qualities as explained in the preceding illustrations.

For men's voices the D-*d* range is generally the best for vocalizing purposes. For mixed voices transpose a half-tone higher, and for women's voices a whole-tone higher. There is a tendency for women's convent choirs in general to chant their Office and sing the songs too high, to the sacrifice of tonal quality. Often nothing other than a half-tone modulation downward produces the desired results of unrestrained singing or chanting. Of course a song pitched too low or an Office chanted too low for given voices is equally faulty. This is where ear training comes in. The choir director should be able to detect whether the pitch of a given song or chanted Psalm is too low or too high for the general range of his singers.

Certainly our efforts to acquire knowledge of our subject as science and art in order that we may better understand and interpret it, is not motivated by a desire to become "technical perfectionists" as such. The supreme motive which spurs us on in our unceasing quest is the aspiration of an ever more perfected rendition of a song composed, studied and rendered uniquely for the service and praise of God, and, as Archbishop Kenrick so profoundly expresses it (Cf. p. 56, Part I), "one that will be learned here and continued before the Eternal Throne."

The Angelic Doctor too has assured us that the divine praise of heaven will be a true song:

In sanctis VOCALIS *laus Dei*

Daily Vocal Exercises on the Dorian Scale

Podatus
For Figure No. 1
Clivis
Scandicus
For Figure No. 2
Climacus
Torculus

Vocal Exercises

Porrectus
Pressus
For Figure No. 3
Pressus
Pressus
For Figure No. 4
Pressus
Salicus
For Figure No. 5

FOOTNOTES

CHAPTER I. THE PSALTER

1. Dr. A. Cohen, *The Psalms* (Soncino Press, London), x; Dr. Michael Seisenberger, *The Study of the Bible* (Wagner, N. Y.), 284; Rev. A. Robert & Rev A. Tricot, *Guide to the Bible*, I (Desclée & Co., Rome) 174.
2. Rev. Walter Drum, S.J., *Catholic Encyclopedia, Psalms.*
3. Quoted from Robert & Tricot, *op. cit.*, 516.
4. *Liber Psalmorum* (Pont. Bibl. Inst., Rome), xv.
5. I *Esd.*, 3:10; II *Mach.*, 2:13.
6. Robert & Tricot, *op cit.*, 177.
7. Rev. A. Alberto Vaccari, S.J., *De Libris Veteris Testamenti* (Rome), II, 9.
8. I *Par.*, 16:36.

CHAPTER II. TITLES OF THE PSALMS

1. Quoted from Robert & Tricot, *op. cit.*, 515-516.
2. Rev. Edward F. Siegmen, C.P.P.S., *Catholic Biblical Quarterly*, (Jan., 1956) 23 ff.
3. A. Maclaren, *The Book of Psalms*, quoted from Cohen, *op. cit.*, 297.
4. I *Par.*, 16:41; II *Par.*, 23:18; I *Esd.*, 3:10.
5. *Enchiridion Biblicum*, n. 43.
6. *Ib.*, n. 343.
7. Quoted from Robert & Tricot, *op. cit.*, 516.
8. Rev. R. Tournay, O.P., & Raymond Schwab, *Les Psaumes* (Les éd. du Cerf, Paris), 14, 15, 16, 166.
9. *Num.*, 26; 11:58.
10. II *Par.*, 29.
11. I *Par.* 16:5 ff.
12. I *Esd.* 2:41.
13. I *Par.*, 6: 33-44.
14. Tournay & Schwab, *op. cit.*, 49.
15. *Ib.*, 8.
16. Artur Weiser, *Die Psalmen* (Vanderhoeck & Ruprecht, Göttingen), I, 62.
17. *Ench. Bibl.*, n. 346.
18. Vaccari, *op. cit.*, 14.
19. *Id.;* Cohen, *op. cit.*, 15 ff.
20. Tournay & Schwab, *op. cit.*, 11, 22, 23, 36, 38.

CHAPTER III. CONTENTS OF THE PSALMS

1. Cohen, *op. cit.*, x-xi.
2. Robert & Tricot., *op. cit.*, 178.
3. Tournay & Schwab, *op. cit.*, 16 ff.
4. *Lib. Psalmorum*, xii-xiii.
5. Cohen *op. cit.*, 161.
6. Cf. p. 3.
7. Tournay & Schwab, *op. cit.*, 23-25.
8. *Ib.*, 44, 45, 20.
9. Tournay & Schwab, *op. cit.*, 133. *The Book of Psalms* (Confraternity Ed., St. Anthony Guild, N. J.), [33].
10. *Gen.*, 14.
11. Cohen, *op. cit.*, 371.
12. *Matt.*, 22: 42-44.
13. Tournay & Schwab, *op. cit.*, 31.
14. Cf. *Eph.* 5, 25 ff; *The Book of Psalms* [78]; Tournay & Schwab, *op. cit.*, 32.
15. Cohen, *op. cit.*, 18.
16. Tournay & Schwab, *op. cit.*, 21, 22.
17. *The Book of Psalms* [187].
18. Tournay & Schwab, *op. cit.*, 51.
19. *Sukkah*, 5, 4.
20. I *Esd.*, 7: 6, 7, 9.
21. *Ib.*, 4:1 ff.
22. Robert & Tricot, *op. cit.*, Vol. II, 75.
23. *Isaias*, 30:29.
24. *Matt.*, 26: 30.
25. *Sukkah*, 4, 5.
26. *Tamid*, 7:3.
27. Cohen, *op. cit.*, 304.

CHAPTER IV. THE MUSIC OF THE TEMPLE

1. *Exodus*, 15.
2. *Gen.*, 4: 20, 21, 22.
3. *Ib.*, 31:27.
4. David Ewen, *Hebrew Music* (Bloch Pub. Co., N. Y.), 10.
5. I *Sam.*, 16:23.
6. *Exod.*, 15:20.
7. II *Sam.*, 6:5.
8. *Ib.*, 12.
9. I *Par.*, 16: 4-8, 37-40, 42-43.
10. *Ib.*, 23: 1, 2, 3, 5.
11. II *Par.*, 5: 2, 3-6, 11-14.

FOOTNOTES (continued)

12. *Ps.* 136 (137): 1-4.
13. I *Esd.*, 2:41.
14. *Ib.*, 3: 10-11.
15. II *Esd.*, 12: 27 ff.
16. (H. Holt & Co., N. Y.), 14, 18 ff.
17. II *Par.*, 20: 18-24.
18. II *Esd.*, 12: 45.
19. *Ib.*, 44-46.

CHAPTER V. THE MODES OF SEMITIC MUSIC

1. Quoted from Rudolph Westphal, *Plutarch, Geschichte der alt. und mittelalt. Musik* (Leukart, Breslau), xix.
2. Idelsohn, *op. cit.*, 24-27, 38.
3. Idelsohn, *op. cit.*, 38; Baruch J. Cohon, *The Structure of the Synagogue Prayer* (Reprint from the Journal of the Amer. Musicological Society, vol. 111, no. 1, 1950).
4. Idelsohn, *op. cit.*, 38, 39, 43, 47; Cohon, *op. cit.*
5. Idelsohn, *op. cit.*, 50, 51, 56.
6. *Ib.*, 56, 57, 59, 60.
7. I *Par.*, 15: 22.
8. II *Esd.*, 8.
9. Arthur Friedlander, "Grove's," (The Macmillan Co., New York, 1935), *Hebrew Music.*
10. Idelsohn, *op. cit.*, 36, 103-107.

CHAPTER VI. FORM AND RHYTHM IN THE TEMPLE MUSIC AND THE PSALTER

1. II *Sam.*, 6: 14.
2. Rev. Patrick Cummins, O.S.B., *A Version of the Psalms* (Introduction).
3. Idelsohn, *op. cit.*, 15, 16.
4. *Matt.*, 36: 30.
5. Idelsohn, *op. cit.*, 20, 21.
6. Cath. Ency., *Antiphon in Greek Liturgy.*
7. Cohen, *op. cit.*, 301; *Book of Psalms* [166].
8. *Ib.*, 382; [201].
9. Rabbi Emil Hirsch, (*Jewish Ency.*), *Psalms.*
10. II *Esd.*, 12: 31, 37.
11. *Book of Psalms* [38]: Tournay & Schwab, *op. cit.*, 22.
12. Tournay & Schwab, *op. cit.*, 50, 51, 167.
13. *Ib.*, 52, 53.
14. *Ib.*, 42, 43, 57.
15. Cummins, *loc. cit.*
16. *Eph.*, 5: 18-20.

INDEX

Part I

Aaron, 26, 37
Abraham, 21
Accents, in Hebrew poetry, 49, 50
Acrostic, Psalms, 28
Ada, 29
Adam, 27
Afflante Spiritu, 7
Ai, 52
Akiba, Rabbi, 46
Alexander the Great, 5
Alexandria, 41
Alleluia, 1, 5, 14, 15, 46
Ambrose, St., 31
Amen, 5, 15, 46, 47
Ammonites, 36
Amon-Re, 25
Amraphel, 21
Anenu, 46
Anonymous, authors, 4, 5
Antiphonal Form, in the Temple, 34, 47, 48
  in the Church, 48
Arabia, 40, 46, 49
Arians, 48
Aristotle, 38
Asaph, 4, 5, 11, 32, 33, 36
Ashkenazic, Jews, 40, 41
Assyria, 9, 11
Athanasius, St., 46, 48
Authors, of Psalms, 4, 5, 8 ff.
Augustine, St., 8, 21
Azaveth, 34
Azra, ben, 35

Babylas, St., 48
Babylon, 25
Babylonians, 9, 46
Banaias, 32
Barachius, 11
Benediktinische Monatschrift, 6
Biblical Commission, 3, 6, 7, 9, 12
Books, of the Bible, 5; Chronicles, 5, 15, 43; Ecclesiasticus, 12; Job, 42, 43, 49; Psalms, 9, 21, 42, 43, 46, 47, 55, 56; Proverbs,
42; Pentateuch, 5, 20, 35, 38, 40, 43, 44; Prophets, 41, 43, 44; Samuel, 16, 17; Wisdom, 10; Esther, Lamentations, Ruth, Ecclesiastes, Song of Songs, Esdras, Nehemias, 43
Breviary, Roman, 2, 22, 51

Caesura, 50
Calmet, Dom. A., 10
Canaan, 11
Canon, Scriptural, 2
Canticle, of Canticles, 10, 43; of Ezechias, 13; of Moses, 29, 31, 41
Cantillation, 43
Captivity, 25
Cantor, 44
Cariathiarim, 31, 45
Chaldeans, 12
Chonenias, 42
Church, the Psalter in the, 9, 19, 21, 22, 28, 46, 48, 56
Cobb, W. F., 26
Cohen, Dr. A., 2, 8, 14, 18, 22, 23, 27, 47
Cohon, B. A., 42
Contents, of Psalms, 18-28
Coreites, 4, 5, 11, 22
Council, of Trent, 9
Cummins, Rev. P., 45, 55

Dance, in Jewish ceremony, 45
David, 21, 30-34, 36, 47; author of Psalms, 3-5, 8-11, 21, 22, 34
Decalogue, 20, 35
Deuteronomy, 47
Diaspora, 27
Divino Afflante Spiritu, 7
Division, of the Psalter, 3-5
Dominican, Little Office, 26
Drum, Rev. W., 2

Ecclesiastes, 10, 41, 43
Ecclesiasticus, 12
Egypt, 11, 29, 30, 51, 52
El Amarna, 11, 51

97

Eliazar, Rabbi, 46
Elohim, 4, 5, 15
Enchiridion Biblicum, 6, 7
Esdras, 4, 43, 48
Esther, 43
Ethan, 12
Ethos, 38
Ewin, D., 29, 30
Ezekiel, 10

Feasts, Dedication of the Temple, 32, 34; 9th of Ab, 42; Paschal, 26, 46; of Tabernacles, 16, 45
Form, in Temple music, 45-48; in Psalmody, 52-55; in Church music, 46, 48
Friedlander, A., 43

Gagal, 34
Geba, 34
Genesis, 29
Gradual Psalms, 25, 26

Haftara, 41, 43
Hagiographa, 2
Hallel, 16, 26, 46, 47
Hallelujah, 46, 47
Hazzan, 44
Heman, 11, 32, 33
Hirsch, Rev. Rabbi, 47
Historical, occasions for composition of Psalms, 16, 17
Hoshiana, 46

Idelsohn, A., 35, 38-46
Idithun, 15, 32, 33
Inspiration, 2
Isaias, 43
Israel, 4, 30, 32-34, 36, 37, 49
Israelites, 21, 22, 25, 43

Jabel, 29
Jacob, 29
Jehiel, 32
Jerome, St., 8
Jerusalem, 25, 32, 48
Jews, Ashkenazic, Persian, Sephardic, Yemenite, 40-44
Jeziel, 32
Job, Book of, 42
Josaphat, 36
Juda, 36

Kantor, 44
Kenrick, Archbishop, 56
Kirkpatrick, A. F., 26

Laban, 29
Law, of Moses, 44, 47
Lamentations, Hebrew 41; Church, 42; in poetry, 50

Mass, Proper of, 2; of the Catechumens, 48
Maclaren, A., 8
Macchabees, 4, 12, 15
Magrepha, 35
Mahol, 45
Masoretic text, 2, 3, 8, 12, 15, 49, 50
Megilloth, 43
Meiyana, 42
Melody, type of, 13-15; musical accompaniment, 11-13, 30-36
Messiah, 20, 21
Messianic Psalms, 21, 22
Metre, 49, 50
Midrash, 13
Mishna, 25, 35
Mizmor, 1
Moabites, 36
Modes, Church, Dorian, Hypodorian, Lydian, Phrygian, 40, 41; Greek, Dorian, Phrygian, Ionian, Aeolian, 40-41; Semitic, Job, Pentateuch, Ruth, Ecclesiastes, Prophets, Psalms, Ten Commandments, Song of the Sea, Blessing of Moses, 38-44
Moses, 4, 8, 29, 30, 41
Mount Sion, 25, 26, 32, 33
Musical instruments, 29-37

Nabuchodonozor, "orchestra," 31
Nehemiah, Rabbi, 46
Nehemias, 25, 34, 43, 48
Nethuphati, 34
Numbering, of the Psalms, 3

Obededom, 31

Paralipomenia (Chronicles), 5, 15, 43

98

Part II

100